Killing The President: The Assassinations of Abraham Lincoln and John F. Kennedy

By Charles River Editors

Introduction

THE ASSASSINATION OF PRESIDENT LINCOLN.
AT FORD'S THEATRE WASHINGTON D.C.APRIL 14TH 1865.

The Assassination of Abraham Lincoln (April 14, 1865)

Until April 14, 1865, John Wilkes Booth was one of the most famous actors of his time, and President Abraham Lincoln had even watched him perform. But his most significant performance at a theater did not take place on the stage. That night, Booth became one of history's most infamous assassins when he assassinated President Lincoln at Ford's Theatre in Washington, D.C.

Booth was a member of the prominent 19th century Booth theatrical family from Maryland and, by the 1860s, was a well-known actor. But he was also a Confederate sympathizer who dabbled in espionage, and he was increasingly outraged at the Lincoln Administration. Although Robert E. Lee's Army of Northern Virginia had surrendered days earlier, Booth believed the war was not yet over because Confederate General Joseph E. Johnston's army was still fighting the Union Army, so he and his group of conspirators plotted to kill Lincoln and other top officials in a bid to decapitate the federal government and help the South.

Perhaps not surprisingly, the actor's flair for the dramatic came at a cost to the plot. It took almost no time for the shocked public and the federal government to begin unraveling Booth's conspiracy, which had mostly faltered from the beginning. Following the shooting, America's most famous manhunt commenced, which itself became the stuff of legends. After the shooting, during which it is believed he broke his leg, Booth fled south on horseback, with authorities hot on his tail. 12 days later, while he was at a farm in rural northern Virginia, Booth was tracked down and shot by Boston Corbett, a Union soldier who acted against orders. Eight others were tried for their alleged involvement in the plot and convicted, and four were hanged shortly thereafter as a result of some of the nation's most famous trials.

Killing The President covers the origins of Booth's plot, the assassination, and the eventual capture and killing of Booth, while assessing the aftermath and analyzing the what ifs. Along with pictures of the important people and places, you will learn about the Lincoln assassination and the manhunt for Booth like you never have before.

The motorcade seconds before the assassination

The Assassination of John F. Kennedy (November 22, 1963)

In the annals of American history, few moments have been so thoroughly seared into the nation's conscience that Americans can remember exactly where and when they heard about an earth-shattering event. In the 20th century, there was Pearl Harbor and the assassination of President John F. Kennedy.

November 22, 1963 started as a typical Friday, and many Americans were unaware that President Kennedy was even heading to Dallas, Texas. John and Jackie arrived in Dallas in the morning, with Texas Governor John Connally alongside them and Vice President Lyndon B. Johnson due to arrive later to meet them there. The Kennedys and the Connallys intended to participate in public events later in the day, and Jackie and John were welcomely surprised by the warm reception they received. A public parade was hosted for the President and First Lady that afternoon, and the First Couple rode with the Connallys in an open motorcade en route to a speech Kennedy would deliver later. As they waved to the people lining the streets, around 12:30 p.m. Central Standard Time, Governor Connally's wife turned around to the first couple and said, "Mr. President, you can't say Dallas doesn't love you."

Moments later, the most controversial assassination in American history took place as a series of shots were fired at the motorcade. The indelible images provided by the Zapruder film of Kennedy being hit in the throat and head, followed by Jackie crawling over the backseat toward the trunk are now instantly recognizable. Within minutes, the news of the shooting began to spread from Dallas across the nation, and everyone's worst fears were confirmed when the President was declared dead about half an hour after the shooting.

In the wake of the shooting, Lee Harvey Oswald was arrested, proclaimed his innocence, and was then murdered himself by Jack Ruby two days later. The day after that, the President was given a state funeral and procession. The unbelievable chain of events that took place in those 72 hours understandably left the nation shell-shocked.

Despite countless official and unofficial investigations, the assassination is just as mysterious and confusing as ever, and conspiracy theories continue to run rampant nearly 50 years after the assassination. Was Lee Harvey Oswald a patsy? Was he a lone gunman? Was the assassination ordered by the mob? *Killing The President* chronicles the entire chain of events leading up to the assassination and its immediate aftermath, examines the different conclusions reached by different investigations, and discusses the conspiracy theories and legacy of the assassination. Along with pictures of important people, places, and events, you will learn about the Kennedy assassination like you never have before.

The Lincoln Assassination

Chapter 1: Plotting Against the President

Booth and the Civil War

The presidential box at Ford's Theatre

In November 1863, the Union's fortunes seemed to be on the rise. The victories at Gettysburg and Vicksburg months earlier in July were decisive turning points that would lead to the South's demise. That month Lincoln would travel to Gettysburg to deliver his immortal address, but he also attended a play, *The Marble Heart*, from his box at the newly opened Ford's Theatre in Washington D.C. The lead role was played by one of the country's most famous actors, John Wilkes Booth.

The Booth Brothers acting in Shakespeare's *Caesar*. John Wilkes is on the far left.

At the time, all the public knew about Booth was that he was a dashing actor, well-versed in Shakespeare, and a man so handsome that he constantly received fan mail from women he made swoon. But the man whose favorite Shakespeare role was Brutus had a far more secret side in his life. Booth was a strong Southern sympathizer, even attending the hanging of John Brown after the raid at Harpers Ferry in 1859, and he was an ardent opponent of abolition. On one tour in St. Louis, Booth was actually detained for "treasonous" remarks after he had vocally expressed his desire for Lincoln and the government to go to hell. His partisanship during the war became so bitter that older brother Edwin, who stayed loyal to the Union and wouldn't perform in the South, often avoided confrontation with him.

Booth had a notoriously high sense of self, but he had mostly proved incompetent at anything outside of acting. Booth earned a reputation for having a flair for the dramatic as an actor, and the Southern sympathizer fancied himself a Confederate spy during the early years of the war, at one point using his fame and position as an actor to help smuggle goods into the South past the ongoing blockade. Still, there were plenty of Southerners who had the same resentment of the North and engaged in Confederate activities on a much higher level, and despite Booth's ardent pro-Southern views, he continued to be welcomed and lauded in the North.

It was not until the Election of 1864 that Booth began plotting a daring move. After Vicksburg and Gettysburg had left the Confederacy's hopes of an outright victory in the war looking highly unlikely, the South held out hope that Lincoln would lose his reelection and be replaced by a

Democrat who would end the war and negotiate peace with the Confederates. When Lincoln won reelection, the South's fate looked even direr. Booth had not been a soldier during the war, which frustrated him, and his hatred of Lincoln and the North now convinced him to strike a blow.

The Original Plan

Today Booth's assassination of Lincoln is often the only part of the plot that Americans remember, but in November 1864, Booth's plan did not involve murder.

When Lincoln brought General Ulysses S. Grant east and put him in charge of all armies, Grant, William Tecumseh Sherman (now in charge out west) and the Lincoln Administration changed their military policies to one that resembled total warfare. The North's great advantages in manpower and resources would now be more heavily relied upon to defeat the South.

One of the most important changes was that the Union stopped exchanging prisoners of war, a move clearly designed to ensure that the Confederacy would be harder pressed to fill its armies. Originally President Lincoln had opposed such exchanges, believing that giving wartime rights to the Confederacy implicitly acknowledged their independence, but they had been generally welcomed by both sides from almost the beginning of the war. Captives were exchanged and traded throughout the conflict's first few years. Exchanges were often not equal, but were dependent on the rank of the soldiers being exchanged. For example, a captured general was exchanged for 46 privates. One major was worth eight privates while a colonel was worth 15. The varying ranks of the soldiers, with privates at the bottom and generals at the top, allowed for different proportions of exchanges.

Ending the exchange eventually led to atrocities at prison camps like Andersonville and Camp Douglas in Illinois, but it had the desired effect of starving the South of able soldiers. Booth was particularly outraged by this, which many on both sides considered barbaric and contrary to the rules of warfare. In fact, generals on both sides still continued the exchange without informing their superiors.

Out of this termination of prisoner exchanges came Booth's original plan. The North might not be willing to exchange soldiers, but Booth was sure they'd exchange for the President. Thus, Booth began gathering conspirators for a plot to kidnap President Lincoln and use *him* as a negotiating token to get back Confederate troops. Booth figured the President would be worth a great number of soldiers, which would give the rebels a potentially huge and much needed influx of men. A month before Lincoln's reelection, Booth took a trip to Montreal, which was a hotbed for Confederate espionage at the time, and he spent 10 days there. Historians are still unsure what exactly Booth did while there, but many have since speculated that he discussed kidnap plans with better connected members of the Confederate Secret Service and networks of spies.

Kidnap was still the plan when Lincoln's second inauguration took place on March 4, 1865. Despite his hatred of Lincoln, Booth attended the President's second inauguration in Washington. Along with a crowd of over 50,000 spectators, Booth watched as the President took the oath and now delivered his famous second inaugural address on the steps of the unfinished U.S. Capitol Building. Alongside Booth in the audience were several of his eventual co-conspirators: Samuel Arnold, George Atzerodt, David Herold, Michael O'Laughlen, Lewis Powell and John Surratt. All of the conspirators were either from or lived in the Washington, D.C. area or in Maryland, and all were opposed to President Lincoln and were fervent supporters of Confederate secession. With the exception of George Atzerodt, who was born in Germany, all of the co-conspirators were Americans.

In the same month as the President's inauguration, Booth assembled this group of conspirators came together to discuss politics and the ongoing Civil War, as well as the kidnapping plot. Their most regular meeting place, and their most notorious, was the boarding house of Mary Surratt, a Southern sympathizer who would later be alleged of facilitating Confederate espionage. Her son John was an active conspirator with Booth, and people staying at the boarding house would later tell military tribunals that Mary met with him as well.

On March 15, the group met at Gautier's Restaurant at 252 Pennsylvania Avenue in Washington, just blocks from the White House. There, they discussed a plan to kidnap the President of the United States, send him to the Confederate capitol in Richmond, and hold him ransom until the Union released Confederate troops. Initially, the most realistic option for capturing the President would be to do so while he was in transit. This ensured that his security detail would be more limited than usual, and his travels were likely to be carried out in less densely populated places, ensuring minimal public awareness of the event. This would allow the group to scurry the President away to Richmond, where he could be held for ransom.

Attempting the Kidnap

Two days later, on March 17, St. Patrick's Day, Booth learned that the President was going to head north to attend a play called *Still Waters Run Deep* at Campbell Military Hospital, located in the northern outskirts of Washington. Because Booth was a member of the nation's acting elite, he was privy to private information about public dignitaries, including the President, attending plays in the D.C. area, the very thing that made his plot possible the following month.

Booth informed his fellow conspirators, and they all agreed to go forward with the plan. Because the President's destination was known and his route could be reasonably assumed, the opportunity presented itself as the perfect one. The conspirators thus assembled along the President's route, hoping to intercept him along his way to the evening matinee. The sun was setting on Washington, providing cover to the conspirators in the darkened streets.

The conspirators were waiting for a man who would never show. To Booth's great dismay, the President had changed his mind and no longer planned to see *Still Waters Run Deep.* Instead, Lincoln attended a ceremony at National Hotel for the 140th Indiana Regiment, which was presenting its governor with a captured battle flag. Ironically, Booth was living at that very hotel at the time.

Chapter 2: From Kidnap to Murder

The Capture of Richmond

With the passing of March, the Civil War had seen critical developments. General Grant and the Army of the Potomac had been laying siege to Robert E. Lee's Army of Northern Virginia at

Petersburg since June 1864, gradually stretching Lee's lines and inching their way toward the Confederacy's main railroad hub, which was only miles away from Richmond itself.

Lee's siege lines at Petersburg were finally broken on April 1 at the Battle of Five Forks, which is best remembered for General George Pickett enjoying a cod bake lunch while his men were being defeated. Historians have attributed it to unusual environmental acoustics that prevented Pickett and his staff from hearing the battle despite their close proximity, not that it mattered to the Confederates at the time. And that would have been Pickett's most famous role in the Civil War if not for the charge named after him on the final day of the Battle of Gettysburg.

When the siege lines were broken at Petersburg, that city fell the following day, as Lee began a week long retreat that famously ended with his surrender at Appomattox Court House. On April 3, the Confederate capitol of Richmond fell to Union troops, and days later President Lincoln himself entered the city and even sat at the desk in the Confederate Executive Mansion where Confederate President Jefferson Davis had led the South for nearly the entire war. This was also a significant development for Booth's plot though, because Richmond had been the destination after the conspirators kidnapped Lincoln. Now, to Booth's horror, the President was in Richmond of his own accord. With the city under Union control, where could they bring the President?

Developments in prisoner exchanges had also prompted more fundamental questions among the conspirators. In early 1865, General Grant agreed to resume prisoner exchanges on a man-for-man basis, believing the war was nearing its end. His intended to negotiate exchanges until all prisoners from both sides were released. Capturing the President had been intended to serve as a negotiating piece in discussions over prisoner exchanges, which General Grant had earlier stopped. With exchanges resumed, what purpose was there in kidnapping Lincoln?

The Old Soldiers Home, where the conspirators planned to kidnap Lincoln

Reconfiguring the Plot

Booth's original plan now lay in shambles, and all of the conspirators were now compelled to reconsider their purpose. Richmond was no longer a viable place to take the President, there was no obvious reason to take the President at all since prisoner exchanges were back in action, and the war was clearly nearing its end. Kidnapping the President would do nothing to bring the Confederacy back into existence or save slavery in the South.

Booth didn't care, continuing to hold out hope of a Confederate victory. To understand Booth's rationale, it is important to remember that General Joseph E. Johnston, who Lee famously replaced at the head of the Army of Northern Virginia, still had a sizable army opposing General Sherman's army near the Carolinas. Although Appomattox is generally regarded as the end of the Civil War, there were still tens of thousands of Confederates in the field throughout April 1865, and Jefferson Davis himself was still holding out hope while fleeing from Richmond. Thus, Booth still intended to help the Confederacy somehow.

Two days after Appomattox, Lincoln gave a speech at the White House in which he expressed his desire to give former slaves the right to vote, a policy that would come to fruition through the

13th, 14th, and 15th Amendments. Naturally, such a policy infuriated Southerners, and Booth was so enraged by the speech that he was later alleged to have claimed, "Now, by God, I'll put him through. That is the last speech he will ever give."

On April 11, the other conspirators still believed the conspiracy was about kidnapping Lincoln, and there was dissension in the ranks. Samuel Arnold and Michael O'Laughlen informed Booth of their intention to not participate in any kidnapping of the President. For them, the resumption of the prisoner exchange program and the coming end of the war made holding the President for ransom a moot point. They chose to disassociate themselves of the entire conspiracy.

Everyone else was still on board, but the group as a whole needed to regroup. Kidnapping the President made less sense than it had before, but these conspirators agreed that something still needed to be done. Various plans were thrown around, including John Surratt's thought that blowing up the White House with a bomb would be the easiest and most effective method of dealing with the President. Surratt had connections with Confederate bomb-making experts who he thought could mine the White House and destroy it. This unlikely plot was made even more unlikely when Thomas Harney, the Confederacy's bomb expert who Surratt considered most likely to successfully bomb the White House, was captured by Union forces on April 10.

While Surratt was in Montreal, likely networking with Confederate spies, Booth and the remaining conspirators were still in Washington. Together they devised a more feasible, though also more complicated, plan to assassinate high-ranking members of the federal government. It would take a miracle to save the South, and they figured the chaos that would ensue with a leaderless national government might do the trick. On April 13, Booth and the conspirators met at the Surratt Boarding House and hatched a plan to assassinate Lincoln, Vice President Andrew Johnson, and Secretary of State William Seward, a sinister plot they thought would throw the federal government into disarray at a critical moment in its history.

Given the manner in which the plot changed, it's not surprising that the conspiracy was still riddled with glaring errors. For whatever reason, the plot overlooked Secretary of War Edwin Stanton, who in many respects asserted the most authority in the wake of Lincoln's assassination before the government began functioning normally again. And Booth pegged conspirator George Atzerodt to be the one to kill Vice President Johnson, even after Atzerodt objected to the murder plots and asked out of the conspiracy.

Now that the conspirators had their new plot, they still needed to figure out when they would carry it out. As fate would have it, they didn't have long to wait.

Atzerodt

Chapter 3: April 14-15, 1865

One of the most decisive days in American history began for Booth at midnight, who found himself wide awake laying in bed. In his diary entry for the day, Booth wrote, "Our cause being almost lost, something decisive and great must be done". But when he woke up, Booth was unaware that the plot would be carried out that night.

Lincoln, on the other hand, slept more than usual. The day was Good Friday, and it was one of the first days in many years that Lincoln was relatively stress free. Though he still had plenty of work to do, its urgency paled in comparison to the decisions he had had to make during the war. After the capture of Richmond and Appomattox, Lincoln now focused more on how to reconstruct the nation than winning the war. At around 8:00 a.m., the President and his son ate breakfast together at a leisurely pace.

Later that morning, he met with many dignitaries to discuss logistics about Reconstruction. He met with Speaker of the House Schuyler Colfax, General Grant, the Governor of Maryland and Senator Creswell, also of Maryland. At 11:00 a.m., the President held a special Cabinet Meeting with General Grant in attendance. Grant relayed intimate details of the surrender at Appomatox to the Cabinet, and the Cabinet discussed what to do about Confederate leaders now that the war had been won. Lincoln hoped they would simply flee the country. Either way, he thought good news was to come, telling his Cabinet that he had a dream the previous night in which he was flying away in some sort of vessel at an indescribable speed. He had had this dream before major victories in the war, and thought it was a harbinger of positive developments. General

Grant, on the other hand, reminded the President that many of the other times the President reported the dream, the Union had lost battles. The President remarked to his Cabinet that, either way, something big was going to happen. Cabinet officials would later note how unusually happy Lincoln was, with Secretary of the Treasury Hugh McCulloch noting, "I never saw Mr. Lincoln so cheerful and happy."

At the end of the meeting, around 2:00 p.m., President Lincoln asked both General Grant and Secretary of War Stanton if they would like to join the Lincoln's at Ford's Theatre later that evening. As it turned out, Stanton and Grant were hearing about Lincoln's plan for the night after Booth had already learned it. Both declined the offer, but Lincoln had already conveyed his plan to bring Grant that night to the people at Ford's Theatre. When Booth stopped by the theater at noon to pick up mail from his permanent mailbox, owner John Ford's brother casually mentioned the president would be attending *Our American Cousin* that night, a play Booth knew so well that he later timed his shooting of Lincoln in conjunction with the play's funniest line, which Booth figured would help him because it would draw the loudest laughs.

Now Booth was set on killing Lincoln during the play. That afternoon he arranged with Mary Surratt to have a package delivered to her tavern in Maryland. Booth had previously stored guns and ammunition at the tavern, and he asked Surratt to inform one of her tenants to have those ready for him to pick up there. It would be this meeting that doomed Mary Surratt to her fate of becoming the first woman executed by the federal government.

After some paperwork, Lincoln and Mary Todd went for a carriage ride throughout the capital, enjoying the fresh air and relaxing environment for nearly two hours. When they returned to the White House, they asked Illinois Governor Richard Oglesby if he wanted to join them at Ford's Theater. He, too, declined. Ultimately, Major Henry Rathbone and his fiancée Clara Harris, the daughter of a New York Senator, accepted the invitation and became Lincoln's guests in the presidential box that night.

Rathbone

At 7:00 p.m., Booth and the other conspirators convened to put the plot in motion. Lewis Powell, a rough and tumble veteran who had suffered a battle wound at Gettysburg, was to break into Secretary of State Seward's home, accompanied by David Herold. There, they were to assassinate the Secretary, who was still weak and recovering from wounds he had suffered in a carriage accident. The same evening, George Atzerodt was to head to the Kirkwood Hotel, where Vice President Johnson was living, and assassinate him as well. All of the attacks were to take place simultaneously around 10:00 p.m., and the conspirators agreed on an escape spot in Maryland to meet up after the attacks.

Between 8:00 and 8:30, the Lincoln's left the White House, and arrived at Ford's Theater shortly thereafter. They were late for the play, which began at 8:00 p.m. A special box on the second story balcony was decorated for the President's arrival, and the Lincolns, Major Rathbone, and Clara Harris settled into their spots and enjoyed the show. They were initially guarded by a policeman, John Frederick Parker, but for reasons that are still unclear, Parker left his post during the middle of the play and headed to a tavern with Lincoln's coachman.

When Booth had heard Grant was attending the play, either he or O'Laughlen followed Grant, who was boarding a train to head to Philadelphia, not Ford's Theatre. It's believed that O'Laughlen attempted to attack Grant that night, but Grant and his wife were too heavily protected by staff onboard the train, and the car they were riding in was locked.

The Attack on Secretary of State Seward

Seward

Powell

Often lost in the aftermath of Lincoln's assassination is Lewis Powell's unbelievable attack on Secretary of State Seward. In fact, Powell's attack on Seward was the first attack of the night. On the other side of Washington D.C., Seward was in his home still convalescing from a carriage accident on April 5 that left him with a concussion, a broken jaw and a broken arm. One of the most famous aspects of the attack was that Seward was wearing a neck brace, but in fact doctors had put together a splint to help his jaw repair.

Shortly after 10:00 p.m., Powell, dressed as a pharmacist and carrying a revolver and a Bowie knife, knocked on the door of Seward's home. The butler answered the knock, at which point Powell told the butler he needed to speak with the Secretary personally, to instruct him how to take his medication.

The butler let him in, but as soon as he entered, Seward's son Frederick stopped him. Not recognizing Powell, Frederick told him Seward was sleeping and could not be awoken, but just as he said that, Seward's daughter opened a door and told them the Secretary was awake. Powell now knew his location, pointed a gun at Frederick's head, and fired. Luckily, the gun misfired, and after the burly Civil War veteran bludgeoned Frederick with the gun and knocked him out cold, the gun was broken.

Powell wouldn't be able to shoot Seward, but he still had the Bowie knife. After knocking out Frederick, Powell rushed wildly into Seward's room and began stabbing at Seward's neck and face, knocking him out of the bed and onto the floor. When Seward's daughter screamed, it awoke Seward's other son, Augustus. Together with the sergeant on detail there, the two began wrestling with Powell, who still managed to stab them and Seward's daughter as they tried to fight him off.

After stabbing those three, Powell fled the scene, only to run directly into a messenger with a telegram at the door. Powell stabbed him in the back and exited the house, only to find that co-conspirator David Herold had abandoned him and fled when he heard the commotion coming from the house. Powell left the scene on horseback, but he had no clue how to get to the meeting spot in Maryland and instead began hiding out in Washington D.C.

Seward had been badly wounded, but not fatally. The jaw splint had deflected Powell's stabs away from the jugular vein, and Seward would go on to recover.

The Assassination of Lincoln

While Secretary of State Seward was under attack, Ford's Theater was in still in the middle of *Our American Cousin*. Booth had suggested the attacks take place around 10:00, but he entered the theater just before 10:30. Because he was a well-known and widely admired actor, no one thought twice about letting him in. Admissions simply assumed he was interested in viewing the play. Moreover, nobody would have thought twice about granting Booth access to Lincoln's presidential box, even if the guard had been in his proper position.

Just at 10:30, the play was at Act III, Scene II, and the actor Harry Hawk was alone on the stage when a gunshot echoed across the theater. The President's bodyguard was absent, having ambled across the street to the nearby tavern. Without having to worry about the bodyguard, Booth was able to penetrate the double-doors of the President's box easily, and he barricaded the first door behind him with a stick so that the President could not escape.

Booth knew *Our American Cousin* by heart, having seen it numerous times. He waited between the doors until Hawk uttered the funniest line of the play. When the audience erupted in laughter, Booth made his shot, striking the President in the back of the head. The President slumped forward, and Mary immediately began screaming while grabbing the back of his shirt.

The pistol Booth used.

At this time, Mary Lincoln, Rathbone and Clara Harris were still the only ones who were aware the president had been shot. As Lincoln slumped forward, Rathbone lunged at Booth to try to stop him, but Booth pulled out his knife and stabbed Rathbone twice before jumping out of the balcony down to the stage, about 12 feet below. It is widely believed that Booth suffered a broken left leg during the jump when his foot got entangled in the flag decorating the box. Always the showman, Booth got up to his feet, crossed the stage, and reportedly yelled "Sic semper tyrannis", which was Virginia's state motto and Latin for "thus always to tyrants."

The crowd was still in a state of confusion while Booth made his last appearance on stage, but Mary and Rathbone were yelling out "catch that man," at which point the audience realized that the excitement was not part of the play. Some members ran towards Booth, but no one was able to capture him, and Booth was able to hop onto the horse he had waiting for him outside and escape.

Having likely suffered a broken leg, Booth knew his part of the assassination plot hadn't gone directly according to plan, but he had no way of knowing just how poorly the rest of it had gone. Herold and Powell had been separated, with Powell failing to kill Seward, but even that was more of a success than George Atzerodt's attack on Vice President Andrew Johnson. This is because that attack never took place. Atzerodt, who Booth insisted on tabbing for the attack on Johnson despite his objections to murder, had lost his nerve while drinking at the Kirkwood's hotel bar. Instead, the drunk Atzerodt roamed the city's streets that night, but only after he had asked the bartender about Johnson, which obviously drew suspicion when news of the attacks on Lincoln and Seward spread. The next day, police searched the room Atzerodt had booked and found a revolver and Bowie knife.

The Death of Lincoln

After the shooting, a doctor in the audience named Charles Leale rushed towards the President's box, only to find that Booth had sealed the door. Together with another doctor in the audience, Charles Sabin Taft, the two men assessed the President's state. He had no pulse, and at first Leale believed him to be dead. The two doctors unbuttoned the President's shirt to try to find the bullet hole before discovering the bullet had entered the back of the President's head. Leale removed blood clots from the hole, which helped Lincoln start to breathe better.

Regardless, both doctors immediately believed the President's wound was mortal and that he would not recover. The two men, together with another Doctor Albert King, consulted on the state of the President. They agreed it was best for him to die in comfort, and not in the box in the theater. However, a bumpy carriage ride back to the White House, which would almost certainly draw a crowd, was not a reasonable option.

The three doctors and some soldiers in the audience carried the President's body across the street, where Henry Safford told them the President could stay in his residence. A bed was prepared, though the President was too tall and needed to lay on it diagonally. At this point, the Petersen House became the de facto headquarters for the federal government and the manhunt for Booth, who had already been immediately identified as the assassin by the time he exited the theater.

The Petersen House

Presidential physicians, including the Surgeon General and Lincoln's personal doctor, arrived to assess the state of the President. They all agreed that the President would not survive.

At this point, news of the shooting began to spread, with Secretary of the Navy Gideon Welles and Secretary of War Stanton rushing over to the Petersen House to all but take control of the federal government. Understandably, Lincoln's wife Mary was a complete wreck, sobbing so loudly that Stanton at one point ordered people to remove her from the room. Indeed, when they arrived, the situation was as grave as they were told, and doctors thought the President would survive for only a few more hours. Physicians, including Canada's first African-American doctor, Anderson Ruffin Abbott, continued to work on the President throughout the night, but the hemorrhaging of his brain could not be stopped.

The following morning, at 7:22 a.m., President Lincoln died, surrounded by Senator Charles Sumner, Generals Henry Halleck, Richard Oglesby and Montgomery Meigs, and Secretary of War Stanton. Mary was not present; she was too distressed throughout the night to see the President. As Lincoln took his last breath, legend has it Stanton famously said, "Now he belongs to the ages." (Other historians speculate he said, "Now he belongs to the angels.")

Stanton

Chapter 4: The Manhunt for Booth

Herold

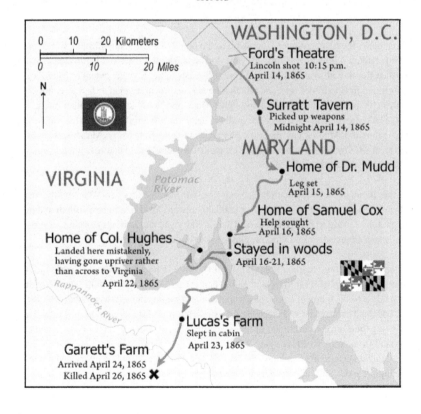

Booth's and Herold's Escape

Given the lack of technology and the delays caused by the shock of Lincoln's assassination, the manhunt for Booth and the unraveling of the conspiracy occurred extremely quickly. Much of the conspiracy was done in by bumbling errors made by the men who didn't escape, while the manhunt for Booth was greatly aided by his broken leg. It is widely believed that Booth suffered a broken leg jumping from the presidential box after shooting Lincoln. If not, it's likely that he suffered a broken leg during the ride out of Washington. Either way, what is clear is that Booth was hampered by a broken leg before the night of April 14 ended.

Despite being in great pain that made horseback riding nearly unbearable, Booth managed to escape, as planned, to Maryland shortly after the shooting. So did David Herold, who had left Powell at Seward's house while Powell was still trying to kill the Secretary of State. The two met up at Mary Surratt's tavern in Surrattville, Maryland, where they picked up supplies, including a revolver, to assist in their escape. These included the materials Booth had told Mrs. Surratt to ensure would be there.

From there, the two continued southward to the home of a Dr. Samuel Mudd, where they arrived at about 4:00 a.m. on April 15. The doctor set Booth's fractured leg in a cast, and he furnished Booth with crutches. Controversy still exists today over the extent of Mudd's involvement in Booth's escape, and whether he was an unwitting plan or had foreknowledge of Booth's conspiracy. Although it is known that Mudd and Booth knew each other dating back to 1864, Mudd proclaimed his innocence until his death, but Atzerodt later told federal investigators that Mudd knew about the plot ahead of time. Either way, Mudd waited until Sunday, April 16, to get word to authorities that Booth and Herold had been there, which ultimately made investigators suspicious.

Within hours of the assassination, Secretary of War Stanton began coordinating the manhunt with authorities. In addition to posting a $100,000 reward for the capture of Booth and his co-conspirators, federal troops had dispersed across Maryland and northern Virginia in search of them, while an investigation of accomplices ensued in Washington.

After spending more than half of April 15 at Dr. Mudd's home, Booth and Herold hid in the swamps and woods of rural Maryland along their escape route to the South. The following day, they made it to the home of a mutual friend, Samuel Cox, in southern Maryland, who helped them contact Thomas Jones. Jones was a Confederate spy who agreed to assist the two in navigating their escape. From there, Jones escorted the two through the woods of southern Maryland from April 16-21, but they did not travel much distance in that time, which would prove crucial because the manhunt was bearing down on them. Booth's injury had made traveling great distances too difficult.

Once the two crossed the Potomac, they crossed the farmland of Virginia, settling down in various farms along the route. By April 24, 10 days after the assassination, the pair made it to Garrett's farm. Incredibly, the family was still unaware of Lincoln's assassination, making it possible for Booth to convince the family that he was an injured Confederate soldier who had trekked through the woods of Virginia for days in search of help.

Unbeknownst to them, federal authorities were closing in on them. The manhunt naturally assumed that Booth would be heading south from Washington D.C., where he would be more likely to find sympathizers and aid in the Southern states. When they found out Mudd had set his leg, it confirmed a southern route.

Still, the federal authorities and soldiers pursuing Booth had no clue where he was on April 25. Lieutenant Edward P. Doherty, who was leading the 16th New York Cavalry, later wrote in his official report that they only "had reliable information that the assassin Booth and his accomplice were somewhere between the Potomac and Rappahannock Rivers." That day, while interrogating men near a ferry spot, the 16th New York Cavalry learned that men matching Booth's and Herold's descriptions had crossed via that very ferry the day before on their way to the house of a Mr. Roland. Moreover, they learned that Booth and Herold had tried to hire someone to take them to Bowling Green, which as it turned out was 12 miles away from Garrett's Farm.

Booth met his fate early on the morning of April 26, when Doherty's unit of about 30 men surrounded Garrett's Farm and quickly learned from Mr. Garrett that Booth and Herold were in the barn. Doherty explained what happened in his official report:

Sergt. Boston Corbett, Company L, Sixteenth New York Cavalry asked permission to enter the barn alone, which I refused. Booth all this time was very defiant and refused to surrender. At one time he said if we would draw up in line fifty paces off he would come out, adding that he was lame and had only one leg. This, however, I refused. Booth up to this time had denied there was anyone in the barn besides himself. Considerable conversation now took place between myself, Booth, and the detectives. We threatened to burn the barn if he did not surrender; at one time gave him ten minutes to make up his mind. Finally, Booth said, "Oh; Captain, there is a man here who wants to surrender awful bad:" I answered, and I think Mr. Baker did at the same time, "Hand out your arms." Herold replied, "I have none." Baker said, "We know exactly what you have got." Booth replied, "I own all the arms, and intend to use them on you gentlemen."... Almost simultaneous with my taking Herold out of the barn the hay in the rear of the barn was ignited by Mr. Conger, and the barn fired. Sergt. Boston Corbett, Company L, Sixteenth New York Cavalry, shot the assassin Booth, wounding him in the neck. I entered the barn as soon as the shot was fired, dragging Herold with me, and found that Booth had fallen on his back. Messrs. Conger and Baker, with some of my men, entered the barn and took hold of Booth."

The unit had orders not to kill Booth, so the soldiers lit the corners of the barn on fire in order to smoke Booth out. However, when Sergeant Boston Corbett spotted Booth near the back door of the barn holding two guns, he mortally wounded Booth with a shot to the spine. Booth spent the next two hours paralyzed, and shortly before his death, he asked a soldier to hold up his hands. Looking at his hands, Booth uttered his last words, "Useless. Useless."

Although they had intended to take Booth alive, Doherty wrote, "I beg to state that it has afforded my command and myself inexpressible pleasure to be the humble instruments of capturing the foul assassins who caused the death of our beloved President and plunged the nation in mourning." Corbett was actually placed under arrest for disobeying orders, but the charges were dropped at the behest of Secretary of War Stanton himself. Each member of the 16th New York Cavalry collected a share of the reward for Booth's death, receiving over $1,500 each. Over the coming decades, Corbett was so volatile and unstable that he was eventually placed in an insane asylum in the 1880s.

Corbett

The Capture of Atzerodt and Powell

Amazingly, despite being the only one instantly identified as one of the conspirators, and despite being killed less than two weeks after the assassination, Booth was the last of the main conspirators to be captured. It took federal soldiers 12 days to capture Booth and Herold, but it took far less time for Powell and Atzerodt to literally walk themselves into custody.

On the night of April 14, while his co-conspirators were carrying out their attacks and fleeing, George Atzerodt was stumbling around. Atzerodt was supposed to assassinate Vice President (now President) Andrew Johnson, but he got so drunk that he spent the nights walking throughout the city. Apparently, he never spent any part of the night in the hotel room he had booked. However, when Atzerodt asked the bartender where Vice President Johnson was sleeping, the curious question would lead authorities straight to him.

The bartender contacted the police, who were now fully engaged in a city-wide manhunt and investigation. The following day, the military police searched Atzerodt's room, finding a revolver and a bank book belonging to Booth. This was sufficient evidence to warrant arresting Atzerodt. On April 20, George Atzerodt was arrested without a fight, in Germantown, Maryland, where he had been staying with his cousin since leaving the hotel.

Meanwhile, Powell unwittingly unraveled the rest of the conspiracy for authorities. After attacking the Secretary of State, Powell exited the home to find that his accomplice, David Herold, had already fled. Powell was now being chased by Seward's family and neighbors, so he fled the scene on horseback, leaving his weapons behind. Powell fled to a cemetery in a Washington suburb, where he discarded remaining evidence and remained for some time. He hid in a tree there for three days, aware that he was being chased, but unsure of the route to the agreed-upon Maryland meeting location.

Obviously Powell knew he could not hide out in public forever, but without having any clue how to get to a safe place in Maryland, the only viable location he could think of was the boarding house of Mary Surratt, where the conspirators had met on so many occasions.

Powell could not have picked a worse time than the evening of April 17 to reappear at Mary Surratt's boarding house. Through a combination of factors, including the information relayed through Surratt's African-American servants, federal authorities tied Surratt's son John to the attempt on Seward, and they came to believe Mary Surratt was somehow involved in the plot. The boarding house's association with Booth had been attested to by witnesses as well.

When authorities entered her home, Mary denied having any involvement in the plot. She also lied about her son's whereabouts and the fact she had helped Booth arrange to pick up a package at her tavern on April 14. On the night of April 17, as authorities were getting ready to charge her for the conspiracy, Powell showed up at her door in disguise, claiming he was there to dig a ditch. Mary claimed not to recognize Powell, but not surprisingly, the authorities did not believe Powell was there to dig a ditch at night. And given how often Powell was at the boarding house, Mary's claim not to recognize him struck the authorities as yet another lie. Both Powell and Surratt were arrested that night.

Other Arrests

Ironically, Mary suffered a far worse fate than her son, despite the fact he was almost certainly more involved in the conspiracy. John Surratt Jr. also proved to be far more difficult to catch. At the time of the assassination, he was in Elmira, New York, nowhere near Washington, D.C. However, interrogations of arrested conspirators led authorities to believe he was involved in the plot. By then, he had fled to Montreal, Canada, where he was protected by Roman Catholic priests.

Surratt didn't just seek safety north of the border. Eventually, he fled overseas to England, where he assumed the name John Watson. From there, he became nomadic, moving around Europe and North Africa, while federal authorities maintained a warrant for his arrest. He even served briefly in the army of the Papal States, but in November 1866, more than a year after the murder, an old American friend traveling through Italy recognized Surratt and alerted the American Embassy. He was arrested on November 7, and sent to an Italian prison, but managed to escape, and fled to Alexandria, Egypt, where he was again arrested by U.S. authorities on November 23. He was sent home via ship to Washington, D.C., where he was imprisoned in early 1867.

In addition to the conspirators most directly involved in the assassination of the President and the attempted assassinations of Secretary of State Seward and Vice President Johnson, dozens more were arrested on related charges, though many were later released.

Two of the original conspirators, Samuel Arnold and Michael O'Laughlen, were both arrested, despite backing out of the plot when it turned into an assassination scheme. Arnold was arrested in Fortress Monroe, Virginia, after authorities found correspondence between him and Booth that pertained to a plot against the government. Arnold proved especially critical to the government, as he had backed out of the plot and was willing to give extensive information to authorities. This information led them to another former conspirator, Michael O'Laughlen. He voluntarily surrendered himself in Baltimore.

In addition to Mary Surratt and Powell, several other important arrests were made on April 17. Among them was Edman Spangler, a Ford's Theatre employee who held Booth's horse in the back of the theater so that the assassin could make an easy escape. The owner of the theater himself, John Ford, was arrested as a suspicious character. A boarder at Surratt's home, and Booth's own brother were also incarcerated. Many others who were tangentially connected to the supply chain of the assassination and escape were arrested, including the stable owner who sold Booth a horse, Dr. Mudd, Samuel Cox and Thomas Jones, who had helped Herold and Booth escape through Maryland and Virginia.

Chapter 5: Trying the Conspirators

Military or Civilian Trials?

The killing of Booth and the apprehension of the conspiracy's main players was remarkably successful, but the means of trying the conspirators, and who to try for what, was an open question among military officials. The events were intimately connected to the Civil War, but they were also carried out by civilians independent of any military body. And though the authorities tried desperately to see if there was a connection between the assassination and the upper reaches of the Confederate government (including the recently captured Jefferson Davis), the inability to find hard evidence connecting Booth to actual Confederates ensured the way to try the people caught was heavily debated. For example, Secretary of War Stanton supported a military tribunal to be followed by executions, but former Attorney General Lincoln Bates favored a civilian trial, believing a military tribunal was unconstitutional given the circumstances.

In the aftermath of Lincoln's death, members of the government worried that a military tribunal and execution of Lincoln's assassins would turn *them* into martyrs. In the long run, it didn't. While the South was not traumatized at all by Lincoln's passing, they were not eager to laud the plot against the federal government. To many, even in the South, Booth's and the conspirators' actions were dishonorable. The South recognized that it had lost, and Booth's actions were viewed as a foolish attempt to save the Confederacy.

To resolve the issue, President Johnson asked sitting Attorney General James Speed to prepare a reasoned brief defending his position on the issue. Speed reasoned that, because the President was assassinated before the complete cessation of the Confederate rebellion, the issue was properly handled by the war department, as it was an act of war against the United States. A military tribunal was thus decided. On May 1, 1865, President Johnson ordered a nine-person military tribunal be set up to try to the alleged assassins. The members of the commission were: Generals David Hunter, August Kautz, Albion Howe, James Ekin, David Clendenin, Lewis Wallace, Robert Foster, T.M. Harris and Colonel C.H. Tomkins.

Holding military tribunals greatly affected the ability of the conspirators to defend themselves. The rules of the commission stipulated that a simple majority vote would lead to a conviction, while a vote of two-thirds or more meant the death penalty. All conspirators were offered legal counsel, if they wanted it, but the tribunal did not assure them basic trial rights afforded by the Constitution either. In particular, evidence like hearsay that would never be admissible in regular trial courts was allowed in the military tribunal.

The Trials

Ultimately, only eight conspirators were charged and tried by the military tribunal: Samuel Arnold, George Atzerodt, David Herold, Samuel Mudd, Michael O'Laughlen, Lewis Powell, Edman Spangler and Mary Surratt. The trials began on May 9, 1865, and lasted for seven weeks, ending on June 30th, 1865. It was held on the third floor of the Old Arsenal Penitentiary.

Photograph of the District penitentiary, about 1865, after it had been taken over by the United States Army for use as an arsenal.

The prosecution team charged with trying to convict the eight consisted of General Joseph Holt, John A. Bingham and HL Burnett, lawyers.

Lewis Powell's trial was the most convincing, since the assassin failed to kill his target and was witnessed by many in the Secretary of State's family. Additionally, the circumstances of his arrest added further evidence against him. Authorities had eye-witness reports against Powell, and he left guns and other belongings behind on his escape route. The best his defense attorney could do was to argue that his life not be taken because he was an insane fanatic. Regardless, Powell was found guilty and sentenced to death by hanging.

The evidence against David Herold was just as incriminating. He was, after all, apprehended in the company of Lincoln's assassin, John Wilkes Booth. Worse, Herold was proud of the crime, and bragged about it throughout the proceedings. His attorney had little hope for saving his client's life, and relied on the argument that Herold was a simpleton, too stupid to realize the gravity of his crime, and that his life should therefore be spared. The military tribunal didn't buy the argument and sentenced Herold to death by hanging.

The remaining defendants were not so easily prosecuted. George Atzerodt had not killed anyone, and explicitly said he was not interested in doing the job. Regardless, his hotel room showed correspondence with Booth and he had a gun under his pillow, suggesting he second-guessed his reluctance to kill the Vice President. His defense attorney used his cowardice to try to prevent Atzerodt from receiving the death penalty, noting his client was too cowardly to ever go through with the assassination. However, Atzerodt also took no active steps to stop the murder conspiracy despite his knowledge of it, and he went on the run after April 14 and hid out. The military tribunal eventually decided that he, too, deserved death by hanging.

Mary Surratt

Mary Surratt was the last and most controversial defendant to receive a conviction of death by hanging. Just about everyone believed she facilitated the conspiracy in critical ways, from the use of the boarding house to ensuring Booth could pick up supplies from her tavern, but did she know the intent of the conspiracy or play an active enough role to warrant death? Her culpability was rarely doubted, but she was among the most hotly defended. More witnesses testified on her behalf than any other defendant, and due to the nature of her involvement aiding and abetting the assassins, hers was a more evidence-intensive trial. The government relied on witnesses to attest that she had conspired with the assassins, including being present in meetings held by Booth and the other major conspirators. Meanwhile, her attorneys tried to portray Surratt as a woman loyal to the Union, who would not support killing the President. They also tried to impeach the testimony of the people who testified against her, including neighbors and servants, and knock out their testimony as unreliable. However, all of these defenses were undermined by the fact that, in the moments of her arrest, Powell came to her home with weapons and a clear intent to hide out. And her claim that she did not recognize Powell that night, despite the fact he had frequently met other conspirators in her boarding house, greatly damaged her believability. Although Powell would tell authorities Surratt was completely innocent, Atzerodt told authorities she was more deeply involved in the conspiracy than even authorities believed. Eventually she was thus convicted and sentenced to death by hanging. When President Johnson signed her death warrant, he is said to have remarked she "kept the nest that hatched the egg".

The remaining four defendants did not receive death sentences. Dr. Samuel Mudd, who set Booth's broken leg, was charged with aiding Booth in his escape. His defense focused on Mudd's being a Union man who treated his slaves well. Others testified against this, arguing that Mudd was indeed a Confederate sympathizer. Even still, authorities could prove no connection to the conspiracy other than the fact Mudd helped an injured Booth in the middle of the night on April 15, not exactly the most damning evidence. Mudd barely escaped the hangman, avoiding the death penalty by one vote, and was instead sentenced to life in prison. His guilt, however, was endlessly doubted, until President Johnson pardoned the doctor on March 8, 1869, in part because he had served ably as a doctor during a yellow fever outbreak at the prison in Fort Jefferson.

Dr. Mudd

Samuel Arnold's and Michael O'Laughlen's trials were very similar to the prior ones pertaining to aiding and abetting the assassins. Because they did not directly participate in the attacks, their trials focused on their loyalty to the Union and reluctance to kill. Those defenses spared them the death penalty, but not life in prison. Like Mudd, Arnold was pardoned in 1869, but O'Laughlen died of yellow fever in 1867 while at Fort Jefferson.

Finally, Edmund Spangler, who had watched Booth's horse while he shot the President, was given the lightest sentence of the eight, at six years in prison. The evidence against him was highly questionable, as many were uncertain that he knew the purpose of watching Booth's horse was to kill the President. Spangler allegedly thought the horse was poorly tamed, and simply needed someone to keep an eye on it. Because of this, he was only sentenced to six years in prison. He served a shorter sentence, however, when President Johnson also pardoned him in 1869.

Hangings and Imprisonment

Because the eight had been sentenced by military tribunal, the Commander-in-Chief needed to give his ultimate seal of approval before action could be taken. When the trial ended on June 3[h], the Commission forwarded its report to President Johnson, who signed the death warrants. It marked the first time a woman had been sentenced the death penalty by the U.S. government, a step that alarmed even some of the judges of the tribunal, who asked Johnson to commute Surratt's death sentence.

Mary Surratt's lawyers hurried together a review to be done in lower courts, but President Johnson quashed the review, saying that a military tribunal sentence could not be appealed in civilian courts.

On July 7, 1865, Union General Winfield Scott Hancock brought the four convicted assassins to the Old Arsenal Penitentiary in Washington, D.C., around noon. At 1:30, the trap underneath the hanging four was removed, and Mary Surratt, George Atzerodt, Lewis Powell and David Herold fell to their deaths.

The death warrants are read before the hangings.

The execution of Mary Surratt, Powell, Herold, and Atzerodt

In August 1867, John Surratt was brought back to the United States from Egypt, where he was tried in a civilian court. The jury was hung on his case, and he was thus not guilty. He was released from prison and began a speaking tour, detailing the conspiracy across the nation. Despite almost certainly being more involved in the conspiracy than his mother, Surratt lived out the rest of his life a free man.

Apart from Michael O'Laughlen, who died in prison, the remaining conspirators were released by President Johnson in an eleventh hour pardon before he left office in early 1869. The President's pardons outraged the North. Not only did he pardon the assassins, but he also pardoned high-ranking members of the Confederacy, and offered excessive clemency.

Chapter 6: The Aftermath and Legacy of the Lincoln Assassination

Lincoln's Funeral

Abraham Lincoln was not the first president to die in office, nor the first president to be shot at (an assassin tried to kill President Andrew Jackson nearly 30 years earlier). But he was the first

American President to be assassinated.

After the President's death, his body was moved to the White House, where he lay in state in a temporary coffin. There, the President's body was prepared for burial. A public viewing took place from 9:30 a.m. until 5:30 p.m. on April 18th, which was followed by a private viewing for two hours afterwards. A short, private service was held in the Green Room.

Funeral procession in Washington

From there, the Lincoln Funeral in Washington, D.C., began on April 19 at 2:00 p.m., when the President's body left the White House for the last time, and travelled down Pennsylvania Avenue to the Capitol Rotunda. Six gray horses carried the President's coffin. Despite an enormous crowd, the procession was nearly silent, except for a dim drumming and the sounds of the horses' hooves. Once the procession reached the Capitol, the President's body was escorted up the very steps on which he was inaugurated less than two months earlier. The coffin was brought into the Capitol Rotunda, where his body remained alone overnight.

The following day, the Rotunda was opened for a public viewing of the President. At around 7:00 a.m., the public began flowing through the Capitol, with a steady stream coming through consistently until the sun began to set.

On April 21, the President's body finally left Washington, for the beginning of a long train route back to Illinois. The train embarked on a nationwide viewing, which began in nearby Baltimore, Maryland. From there, the train moved on to the following sites: Harrisburg, Pennsylvania; Philadelphia; New York City; Albany, New York; Buffalo; Cleveland; Columbus, Indianapolis; Michigan City, Indiana; Chicago; and, finally, Springfield, Illinois. The President's body lay in state at each location.

Lincoln's funeral was, and still is, widely regarded as the greatest funeral in the history of the United States. Never before, or since, has a single person passed through so many communities: though the President's body only rested in state in the previous communities, the funeral train passed through over 400 towns and cities.

Once in Springfield, the President lay in state a final time before being brought to the Oak Ridge Cemetery for burial. Alongside his son William Wallace Lincoln's body, the two were moved to a receiving vault on May 4th, 1865. The Lincoln Tomb was still under construction, and would not be complete for some years, when Lincoln was relocated.

Being the first American President assassinated, President Lincoln's death shook the nation to its core. After four years of unprecedented trauma, Lincoln had guided the nation through the Civil War, only to become in some ways one of its last victims. On May 23-24, to commemorate the end of the war, regiments of the Union Armies held a Grand Review of the Armies, parading through the streets of Washington D.C. Famous leaders like Generals Sherman and Grant were present, as were the government's top officials, but Lincoln's absence could not help but be felt by everyone.

Still, it's necessary to remember that his untimely death transformed him into a martyr and dramatically altered his legacy in American history. At the time of his death, Lincoln's image transformed overnight. On April 14, Lincoln was a solid, but controversial, President. For much of his presidency, he was under attack from all sides: Democrats considered him a power grabber disregarding the Constitution, Republicans didn't like his policy plans for Reconstruction, many didn't respect the Westerner they considered to be too coarse, and the South despised him. Put simply, Lincoln may have been appreciated among freed blacks in the South and people in the North for leading the nation through the Civil War, but he was not the titanic figure he is today.

However, in the generation after the Civil War, Lincoln became an American deity and one of the most written about men in history. Furthermore, the gravity of his legacy skyrocketed on the morning of April 15. The tragedy and unexpectedness of his death, coupled with its violence, helped turn Lincoln into a martyr, and Lincoln's accomplishments were solidified. Lincoln had ended slavery in the South and ensured that the Union remained undivided. He had also put in place Reconstruction policies that would help lead to sectional reconciliation and the Civil War

Amendments, which ended slavery, gave minorities voting rights, and provided equal protection of citizens against the actions of the states. Without question, these accomplishments earned Lincoln a place in the pantheon of American legends.

At the same time, Lincoln had clearly reached the apex of his presidency with the defeat of the Confederacy. With a second term fully ahead of him, there's no telling how mired his legacy would have been by Reconstruction, which pitted Radical Republicans against President Johnson and Democrats. The Republicans wished to subject the South to harsher treatment than Johnson's conciliatory policies, and even though many in the South were allowed to take loyalty oaths, many continued to intimidate, suppress, and kill blacks, remaining "unreconstructed". Eventually, the South was put under martial law and turned into military districts put under the control of the federal army. Reconstruction would not officially end until 1876, and while there's no question that Lincoln would have governed more competently than Andrew Johnson, there's also no question that Reconstruction during his second term would have tarnished his record, and ultimately, his legacy.

Nevertheless, those alternatives remain what ifs, and historians today widely consider Lincoln the country's greatest President. There is equally little question that his assassination helped propel him to that position. With his tragic death, the aura of martyr would not surround Lincoln, and his record might have looked far different if he left office in 1868. The Abraham Lincoln we know today owes its origins to the events of April 14, 1865, and the hands of one man: John Wilkes Booth.

Bibliography

Deeb, Michael J. *The Lincoln Assassination: Who Helped John Wilkes Booth Murder Lincoln?* Iuniverse.com: 2011.

O'Reilly, Bill. *Killing Lincoln: The Shocking Assassination that Changed America Forever.* New York: Henry Holt, 2011.

Schwartz, Barry. *Abraham Lincoln and the Forge of National Memory.* Chicago: University of Chicago Press, 2000.

The Kennedy Assassination

John and Jackie Kennedy arriving in Dallas the morning of November 22, 1963

Chapter 1: Before Dallas

A Camelot Sized Mirage

In many ways, John Fitzgerald Kennedy and his young family were the perfect embodiment of the '60s. The decade began with a sense of idealism, personified by the attractive Kennedy, his beautiful and fashionable wife Jackie, and his young children. Months into his presidency, Kennedy exhorted the country to reach for the stars, calling upon the nation to send a man to the Moon and back by the end of the decade. In 1961, Kennedy made it seem like anything was possible, and Americans were eager to believe him. The Kennedy years would be fondly and famously labeled "Camelot" during an interview given by the recently widowed Jackie Kennedy shortly after her husband's assassination, suggesting an almost mythical quality about the young President and his family. Much of the glamor and vigor of Camelot, if not the majority of it, was supplied by the former First Lady, whose elegance and grace made her the most popular woman in the world. Her popularity threatened to eclipse even her husband's, who famously quipped on one Presidential trip to France that he was "the man who accompanied Jacqueline Kennedy to Paris."

As it turned out, the decade would reflect both the glossy and idealistic portrayal of John F. Kennedy, as well as the uglier truths of the man and his administration. The country would achieve Kennedy's goal of a manned moon mission, and the landmark Civil Rights Act of 1964 finally guaranteed minorities their civil rights and restored equality, ensuring that the country "would live out the true meaning of its creed." But the idealism and optimism of the decade was quickly shattered by the President's own assassination. The rest of the decade would be marred by the Vietnam War, and by the time Robert F. Kennedy and Martin Luther King, Jr. were assassinated in 1968, the country was irreversibly jaded.

It was only natural that the mythology surrounding the President and his administration would bloom in the wake of his tragic death, but it has also obscured the political realities of 1963 and the reason John F. Kennedy was even in Dallas on that fateful day.

The Election of 1960

Kennedy's assassination has frozen him in time as the image of a youthful President seemingly capable of anything, but his election in 1960 and the first few years of his presidency had been a political dogfight.

At the start of the campaigning for the Democratic Party's nomination, a poll of Congressional Democrats ranked Senate Majority Leader Lyndon B. Johnson at the top for the nomination, followed by Adlai Stevenson, Stuart Symington, and John F. Kennedy. Back in 1960 it was conceivable that a candidate could skip the primaries entirely and then rely on the party establishment at the convention to make them the nominee. Senator Johnson thought the primaries were risky business, since losing one would signal that a candidate was not viable among voters and extinguish any hope of winning the nomination, and he felt he didn't need to take this risk. Senator Kennedy, on the other hand, thought a victory in the primaries would make it hard for delegates to deny the nomination to that candidate. Privately, John and his father Joe had discussed the 1960 Presidential Election since Kennedy's Vice-Presidential hopes in 1956. John thought his Catholicism was the biggest barrier to the Presidency, while his father thought otherwise. To Joseph Sr., the nation had grown beyond its anti-Catholic sentiments and was ready to accept a Catholic President. Furthermore, since the 1956 Convention, the media had viewed Senator Kennedy as the frontrunner for the Democratic nomination. Polls of Democratic voters confirmed this view, showing Senator Kennedy in a tie with former nominee Adlai Stevenson for the 1960 nomination.

As Kennedy's campaign anticipated, the candidate succeeded in the primaries that Johnson chose to abstain from. Throughout the few primaries that were conducted that year, John had the opportunity to prove his broad appeal to the Convention's party elders, and his win in the largely white and Protestant state of West Virginia seemed to amply prove his claim that he did not just appeal narrowly to fellow Catholics. This gave the convention little reason to deny Kennedy the nomination, and he was thus chosen over Johnson to be the Democratic candidate for President of the United States.

John preferred Lyndon Johnson as vice President for several political reasons. Electorally, he thought Johnson made sense: being from Texas, he could help balance Kennedy's decidedly New England-centric appeal. Additionally, Johnson was much older than the youthful Kennedy, which would help deflect concerns about the candidate's age and inexperience. And in the realm of governing, Johnson was a veteran in Washington, having risen to the position of Senate Majority Leader and becoming one of the most powerful wielders of power in the history of that body. Johnson's experience would prove critical in governing the nation, as he had the connections and know-how that John Kennedy admittedly did not. Moreover, much as LBJ had tried to balance the differences in his party over Civil Rights, Kennedy was worried the issue would break his chances of winning the general election. Picking a Southerner like Johnson allowed him to allay the concerns of Dixiecrats and Southern Democrats.

John's brother Bobby, however, was not convinced that Johnson was a good selection. Candidly, Bobby thought Johnson was an intellectual lightweight, an accusation that was not only way off the mark but also clearly tinged with sectionalist prejudices. Bobby, from Massachusetts, thought the Texas Senator was wholly unintelligent. When John called Johnson to ask him to be the Vice Presidential nominee, Bobby reportedly contacted Johnson to ask that he decline the offer. This accusation has never been confirmed; however, it is known that Johnson contacted John again to confirm that he had actually been offered the nomination. Upon hearing it straight from the horse's mouth, he accepted the Vice Presidential nomination.

In the general election, Kennedy and Johnson faced Vice President Richard Nixon and Former Senator Henry Cabot Lodge, who John had defeated for the Senate seat in Massachusetts 8 years earlier. To open the campaign, Kennedy gave his famous New Frontier Speech at the Democratic Convention. In it, he branded his forward-looking ambitions for the United States. Johnson's role in the campaign proved to be exactly what Kennedy intended. The Vice Presidential candidate campaigned diligently throughout the South, especially in his native Texas, which held a significant chunk of electoral votes that would be critical on Election Day. At the same time, the state was not part of the "Solid South," and was something of a swing state: it voted for Truman and Eisenhower in the three preceding elections.

By November, the gap between the two candidates was paper thin. Kennedy remained strong among "white ethnics," labor and African-Americans, while Nixon appealed to rural Protestants, the West Coast, and parts of the South. On Election Day, the popular vote was as close as polls suggested: Kennedy won by a hair, with 49.7% to Nixon's 49.5%. The Electoral College vote, however, was a different story, with Kennedy winning with 303 votes to Nixon's 219. The vote was so close that many still accuse Kennedy and his surrogates of fixing the election, with charges of fraud clouding matters in Texas and Illinois. Nixon would later be praised for refusing to contest the election, but in the following decades it was made clear how much his surrogates had tried to overturn the election.

Johnson's influence had proven critically significant. In some states, he proved to be the critical margin of difference. This included his home state of Texas, which the Kennedy-Johnson ticket carried by just about 2 percentage points. In other Southern states, Johnson merely ensured that the Republicans made no surprise gains. The Johnson factor was probably critical in a state like Arkansas, which the Democratic ticket won by just over 7 percentage points. The "Solid South," despite Johnson, was not as solid in 1960 as it once was: the entry of Harry Byrd as a third party candidate took up some of the South's electoral votes in Alabama and Mississippi. Without Johnson, perhaps other states would have thrown their votes to the third party candidate.

The Election of 1960 demonstrated the various potential political pitfalls that awaited the Kennedy Administration and his reelection campaign in 1964. He had barely managed to win the election in 1960, and the issues that nearly fractured his party, particularly the Civil Rights Movement, would dominate headlines in 1962 and 1963.

A Rough Start

From the very beginning, Kennedy's presidency was an eventful one. The first major crisis came in the form of the Bay of Pigs debacle. In early 1961, just months after his inauguration, Kennedy felt the need to deal with the emerging communist threat that was growing just miles off the US border. Fidel Castro had risen to power less than a decade earlier in the island country, and Castro was forming increasingly strong ties with the Soviet Union. Such an alliance challenged basic US security interests. Hoping to otherthrow the regime, Kennedy approved of a CIA-led plan to invade the country and oust the leader by igniting revolution. Unfortunately, the invasion failed, and Kennedy was left with an international embarrassment.

The failed Bay of Pigs Invasion indirectly led to the next major foreign policy crisis: the Cuban Missile Crisis. The Soviets, hoping to capitalize on a weak and seemingly incompetent US policy, began stationing nuclear missiles in Cuba. These could strike the U.S. homeland, representing an unprecedented threat to the country. For Kennedy, this was unacceptable. Attacking the sites, which represented the easiest way to rid Cuba of missiles, also posed the threat of nuclear war. Diplomacy, however, seemed a longer and more difficult route. After weeks of negotiations, with the world braced for nuclear war, the Soviets agreed to remove the missiles if the US removed its own stationed in Turkey. Nuclear war was averted.

Civil Rights Movement

At home, Kennedy came into office just as the nation was divided on the issue of race. After a 1960 Supreme Court decision in *Boynton v. Virginia*, bus segregation was made illegal on new grounds: it violated the interstate commerce clause of the Constitution, by regulating the movement of people across state lines. With this victory in hand, the Freedom Rides of 1961 began. Organized primarily by a new group – the Congress on Racial Equality (CORE) – the Freedom Rides followed the same guidance that inspired the Montgomery Boycott and the Greensboro Sit-Ins – nonviolent direct action. The purpose of the Freedom Rides was the test the Supreme Court's decision by riding from Virginia to Louisiana on integrated busses. This was notably the first major Civil Rights event that included a large segment of white participants.

Both black and white Northerners had participated in the Freedom Rides, and civil rights activists sought other ways to harness their energy and activism in the next few years. After the Freedom Rides, leaders like Medgar Evers initiated voter registration drives that could help register black voters and build community organizations that could help make their votes count. In February 1962, representatives of various civil rights groups formed the Council of Federated Organizations (COFO), and that Spring they began voter registration organizing in the Mississippi Delta, only to meet fierce resistance from authorities and white-supremacists, including arrests, beatings, shootings, arson, and murder. Similar voter registration campaigns met similar resistance in Louisiana, Alabama, Georgia, and South Carolina. Nevertheless, by 1963 the registration campaigns were widespread and just as crucial as Freedom Rides to integration.

After a drawn out lawsuit, a young man named James Meredith was finally set to attend the University of Mississippi in 1962, a college campus attended by thousands of young men each year. But James Meredith would be no typical young man at the university; he would be its only black man.

As Meredith repeatedly attempted to enter campus that September, he was prevented by a mob, which included Mississippi Governor Ross Barnett. Governor Barnett had earlier attempted to stop Meredith's admission by changing state laws to ban anyone who had been convicted of a state crime. Meredith's "crime" had been false voter registration. An avowed segregationist, Barnett asserted, ""The Good Lord was the original segregationist. He put the black man in Africa. ...He made us white because he wanted us white, and He intended that we should stay that way." And according to Barnett, the reason so many blacks lived in Mississippi at the time was because "they love our way of life here, and that way is segregation." Barnett would later be fined $10,000 and sentenced to jail for contempt (though he never ended up going to jail or paying the fine).

On September 30, Meredith was escorted by U.S. Marshals sent in by Attorney General Bobby Kennedy only to have a white mob attack the marshals, a melee in which nearly 200 people were injured. President Kennedy had to send in the Army to allow Meredith to stay at school. Meredith would receive a bachelor's degree in political science in August 1963. He would later be shot in the back and legs during a civil rights march in 1966 by a white man attempting to assassinate him.

The Civil Rights Movement was in full throttle during the summer of 1963, reaching a crescendo with the March on Washington and Martin Luther King Jr.'s iconic "I Have A Dream" speech on the steps of the Lincoln Memorial, but the Kennedy Administration's relatively tepid support of civil rights was dividing the Democratic Party. Southern conservatives thought Kennedy had proposed too much, while liberals didn't think voting rights went far enough.

Kennedy had originally proposed the Civil Rights Act in the summer of 1963, and both he and Bobby had begun building working relationships with civil rights leaders like Martin Luther King Jr. And prior to his assassination, Kennedy was actively involved in recruiting Congressmen to support the bill. However, the legislation Kennedy supported would not resemble the one passed in 1964 by Lyndon Johnson; it was a limited civil rights act that focused primarily on voting rights but avoided more controversial topics like equal employment and desegregation. Kennedy, of course, had an eye on reelection and was aiming to toe the line between maintaining political support in the South while also holding liberal Democrats. His administration never gained any traction on a Civil Rights bill, with a coalition of Southern Democrats and Republicans preventing any action on one, and Kennedy knew that passage of the bill would be difficult. The legislation seemed certain to languish as Kennedy headed to Dallas with his eye on working toward his reelection.

Midterm Elections

The elections of 1962 represented a test of the popularity of the Kennedy Administration, and up to that point a series of crises had shaken the Kennedy White House. Other issues, including Civil Rights at home, had left many Americans unsure of the President.

The midterm elections that year were almost totally dominated by foreign policy. When political pundits talk about an "October Surprise," there could not be one more consequential or significant than the one that erupted with the Cuban Missile Crisis, which took place from October 16-28, ending just a week before the elections on November 6th. With the world bracing for nuclear war, the ballots cast on November 6th were definitely submitted with that crisis at the fore.

The results of the midterm elections were ultimately balanced. Unlike most midterms, the

President's party did not shed seats in Congress. In the House of Representatives, the Democratic Party maintained resounding control of the chamber by losing just four seats. In the Senate, the results were equally tepid, with the Democratic majority increasing its hold on the body with three seats taken from Republicans.

As a litmus test, however, the midterm elections were certainly no reason for Kennedy to assume his reelection would be certain.

Reelection Prospects

By the fall of 1963, the Kennedy Administration was already gearing up for the following year's Presidential election. The election year was typically full of campaigning and politicking, necessitating a quick and early start.

Though looking back historically always involves many "what ifs," Kennedy's reelection prospects by 1963 were far from certain. His election in 1960 was one of the narrowest victories in history, and a small shift in just a handful of states could have tipped the balance towards the Republicans. There was no reason to think 1964 would necessarily be different.

Kennedy's domestic politics were cautious throughout his term in office. He toed the line on multiple fronts, hoping to maintain a steady hold on the Democratic South, while also maintaining control over the industrial Catholic states. But despite all of his efforts, this Democrats coalition was becoming increasingly tenuous, and the Civil Rights Movement increasingly threatened to tear it apart. The Southern faction and the Northern industrial faction were at odds over the issue of African-Americans for a second time in history, and it seemed the Party's national candidates would eventually need to choose to cater to one or the other. Kennedy consistently looked for ways to not have to make such a choice.

Still, his electoral prospects were hardly lost. Though he personally seemed to attract little extra clout during his presidency, he had a built-in advantage: the Democratic Party itself. Since the days of Franklin Roosevelt, the Party had enjoyed control of Congress and the national government consistently, and there is little evidence that voters particularly disliked Kennedy by 1963. The 1962 elections did not overwhelmingly condemn Kennedy, and polling at the time suggested voters were generally positive about the President, just not overly enthusiastic.

The President was expected to enjoy another advantage in 1964, but one that remained uncertain. By 1964, the Republican Party had a long history of "me too-ism," the idea that the Democratic New Deal policies were so popular that the Republicans should not attempt to oppose them. Instead, the GOP had campaigned throughout the Eisenhower years on an acceptance of the New Deal, adding to it gradually and keeping its fundamentals intact. But a more conservative movement in the early part of the decade led by Arizona's Barry Goldwater threatened to undo Republican acceptance of the New Deal in order to replace it with a hardline conservatism not seen in American politics for over a generation. If Goldwater secured the Republican nomination, few pundits gave him a good chance against Kennedy, and he would indeed suffer a landslide defeat against Lyndon Johnson in 1964.

However, Goldwater's nomination to the Republican ticket was far from set in stone in 1963, and at the time it seemed Kennedy would likely face New York Governor Nelson Rockefeller, a much more moderate candidate who would be palatable to the electorate. There was no way of knowing Goldwater would get the nod in November 1963, and that month President Kennedy had to deal with the fact that he wasn't overly popular nationally. His foreign policy had a number of successes, but Americans had also not forgotten the failures of 1961 and early 1962. Furthermore, his tepid support of civil rights was dividing his own party, between liberals and conservatives. Southern conservatives thought Kennedy had proposed too much, while liberals didn't think voting rights went far enough. Sure enough, the strains would eventually undo the former Democratic coalition of the previous 80 years, done in with the help of Richard Nixon's "southern strategy" in the late 1960s, which saw the South turn solidly Republican at the expense of losing minority support. Lyndon Johnson privately predicted after the Civil Rights Act of 1964 that it ensured the Democrats had lost the South for a generation, and over 40 years later, the South continues to be Republican country in Presidential elections.

Planning a Trip to Texas

President Kennedy was already dealing with this political problem in 1963, and the division was already on display in the state of Texas, where sitting governor John Connally was in conflict with his state's party over the issue. Connally was a former campaign manager for Lyndon Johnson's controversial 1948 Senate campaign, and as a conservative Democrat he was in conflict with liberal Democrats in the state over the issue of civil rights. The Party's division threatened to reduce President Kennedy's chances of carrying the state's absolutely vital 25 electoral votes in the 1964 election. John had made Lyndon Johnson his running mate over the objections of his brother Bobby in 1960 precisely for the purpose of winning Texas that year, which he barely did. It was clear how important Texas was to him, and as part of his reelection efforts the President decided to travel to the state to build support there nearly an entire year before the Presidential election.

Connally

Formally, the purpose of the trip to the Lone Star State in November 1963 was to sew up differences within the state's Democratic Party, but no one doubted that Kennedy hoped to win some votes along the way.

As it turned out, the Kennedy had vocalized the intent to make the fateful visit to Texas all the way back in 1962, and plans for the President's visit were put in place in June 1963 by Vice President Johnson and Texas Governor John Connally. The visit sought to deal with the state Democratic Party's conflict, which threatened to undermine the voter infrastructure necessary to turn out the votes for Kennedy in 1964. Governor John Connally and former opponent and sitting U.S. Senator Ralph Yaborough continued to have feuds over issues of race and economics in Texas, and Kennedy intended to smooth over these issues and reunite the party. Kennedy also hoped to jumpstart his campaign with some fundraising. By stopping in Houston, San Antonio, and Dallas, the President could meet with wealthy party regulars and collect some funds to begin the campaign.

Vice President Lyndon Johnson also had a substantial personal interest vested in the state. As a former U.S. Senator from Texas, Johnson was chosen for the Kennedy ticket in part to deliver the state. He managed that goal in 1960, but if he couldn't in 1964, it would be a significant embarrassment. With political ambitions of his own, being able to deliver it for Kennedy again was crucial, and for that reason Johnson would also be in Dallas on November 22, 1963.

Texas had always been a conservative state, and Kennedy was perceived as precisely the kind of Northeastern liberal Democrat that residents of the Lone Star State still don't favor politically, despite the fact the nation as a whole viewed the President as something of a moderate. Kennedy went to Texas knowing full well that many people there opposed his administration. When Kennedy's Ambassador to the United Nations, Adlai Stevenson, visited Dallas on October 24, 1963, he was met with jeers and was even hit by a sign and spat on. Dallas Police worried that Kennedy would receive similar treatment, and Stevenson personally warned the President about going to Dallas.

WANTED

FOR

TREASON

THIS MAN is wanted for treasonous activities against the United States:

1. Betraying the Constitution (which he swore to uphold):
He is turning the sovereignty of the U. S. over to the communist controlled United Nations.
He is betraying our friends (Cuba, Katanga, Portugal) and befriending our enemies (Russia, Yugoslavia, Poland).
2. He has been WRONG on innumerable issues affecting the security of the U.S. (United Nations-Berlin wall-Missle removal-Cuba-Wheat deals-Test Ban Treaty, etc.)

3. He has been lax in enforcing Communist Registration laws.
4. He has given support and encouragement to the Communist inspired racial riots.
5. He has illegally invaded a sovereign State with federal troops.
6. He has consistantly appointed Anti-Christians to Federal office:
Upholds the Supreme Court in its Anti-Christian rulings.
Aliens and known Communists abound in Federal offices.
7. He has been caught in fantastic LIES to the American people (including personal ones like his previous marraige and divorce).

A handbill that circulated around Dallas on November 21, 1963 accusing President Kennedy of treason.

Just a few days before Stevenson's visit to Dallas, a young man named Lee Harvey Oswald had started working a seasonal job at the Texas School Book Depository.

Chapter 2: November 21, 1963

President Kennedy's trip to Texas began on November 21 with a flight from Washington to San Antonio, where he and Jackie arrived for what was supposed to be a two-day trip. Though he was well aware of the state's rough and tumble political culture, and he was aware of the attack on Adlai Stevenson less than a month earlier, Kennedy was undeterred. In fact, he relished the opportunity to leave Washington for a few days.

In San Antonio, President Kennedy, Vice President Johnson and Governor Connally dedicated the U.S. Air Force School for Aerospace Medicine. The school was a critical part of Kennedy's pledge to put a man on the Moon, so his attendance at the dedication was fitting. Later that day, Kennedy went off to Houston, where he spoke to a Latino-American organization and gave a speech honoring long-serving Congressman Albert Thomas at Rice University. Events like these were intended for public audiences, with political leaders not wanting to give the impression that the President had visited Texas merely to hobnob with important Democratic officials.

Kennedy ended November 21st in Fort Worth, where he slept for the evening. He was scheduled to speak to the area Chamber of Commerce the next morning at the Texas Hotel, and upon waking in the morning, Kennedy was asked to address a crowd that had gathered outside the Texas Hotel. He opted to do so. Standing outside the hotel, despite the cold weather, Kennedy wooed the crowd, and the connection was palpable. Kennedy's off-the-cuff speech got rave reviews in the local press.

After addressing the chamber on the national economy, Kennedy prepared to head to Dallas. He left from Carswell Air Field for what was only a 13 minute flight to Dallas aboard Air Force One. At approximately 11:40 a.m. CST, the President and First Lady were on the ground in Dallas. President Kennedy would be dead about an hour later.

Chapter 3: The Assassination of John F. Kennedy

The labels visible on the image:

County Records building
Presidential Limo's route
Dal-Tex building
County Criminal Courts building
Old Court House
Sniper's nest
Houston Street
Texas Schoolbook Depository
Commerce Street
Zapruder's location
Main Street
Grassy Knoll
Elm Street
Triple Underpass

The motorcade route

Once they arrived in Love Field, President Kennedy and his wife greeted some well-wishers who had gathered to see the President disembark his plane, and Mrs Kennedy even received a bouquet of roses that she carried away with her. The First Couple were more than pleased with the warm reception they received, and Jackie opted to wear a bright pink Chanel suit for the occasion, a conspicuously fashionable choice even for her. Knowing full well that the country and press viewed her every fashion style with interest and fascination, Jackie fully intended to flatter with it.

The President was scheduled to speak at a luncheon at the Dallas Trade Mart, but with the fear that Kennedy's trip might be perceived as too private, the trip to the Trade Market was done to give him maximum public exposure. Thus, a public parade had been conceived for the President, and it was meant to be a lively affair. The President, First Lady, Vice President, Governor Connally and his wife would all drive through the streets of Dallas in this brief parade. Originally, the plan for the motorcade route was to simply stay straight on Main Street instead of turning onto Houston, but because Elm Street was the only way for the motorcade to reach the freeway from Dealey Plaza, the route was changed. Furthermore, if the motorcade stayed on Main Street, it would not offer as many people a chance to see the President publicly. Had the motorcade stayed on Main Street, it never would have been a target from the School Depository Building.

Leaving from Love Field, the President's motorcade consisted of seven vehicles. The first, a white convertible, contained the Dallas sheriff and some Secret Service agents. The second vehicle in the motorcade was the presidential limousine. In the presidential limousine, the Kennedys sat in the back seat, which was elevated a bit higher than the seats in front of them, where Governor Connally and his wife were sitting. A driver and another Secret Service agent were also in the limousine. The third vehicle included aides and Secret Service agents, the fourth had the Vice President, Lady Bird Johnson and Senator Yarborough, and the fifth car had more agents. The last two cars were for members of the press.

At about 11:40 a.m., the President's motorcade departed Love Field, en route for the Trade Mart. The event was running about 10 minutes late due to the crowds that greeted the President at the airfield. Things had gone so well in his meetings with Democratic officials and in the reception they had received that President Kennedy chose to keep the Presidential limousine's top down, in order to feel more connected to the public that had lined the streets in anticipation of seeing the motorcade drive by. In fact, at two points on the route, the motorcade stopped so the President could shake hands with a group of nuns and schoolchildren.

Once the President's motorcade entered Main Street, it continued for a few moments before making a right turn onto Houston Street at about 12:29 p.m. As the motorcade turned onto Houston Street and entered Dealey Plaza, Governor Connally's wife turned around to Kennedy and said to him, "Mr. President, you can't say Dallas doesn't love you." Curiously, as the motorcade moved slowly down Houston Street, it was actually approaching a sniper's nest that had been set up on the sixth floor of the School Depository Building. Conspiracy theorists would later point out that the sniper's nest had a better view and thus an easier shot at the President as his motorcade slowly came toward the School Depository Building on Houston, thus making it inexplicable that a sniper from that position would wait for the motorcade to turn onto Elm Street and start moving away from the shooter.

Dealey Plaza, with the School Book Depository Building in the background and Elm Street in front of it.

Less than a minute later, it became clear that at least one person in Dallas did not love the President. As the motorcade made its way to Elm Street, it made a left turn onto Elm Street that brought the vehicles to a slow crawl. At approximately 12:30, as the motorcade started to slowly head down Elm Street, a number of shots rang out.

The view of Elm Street from the "sniper's nest" in the School Book Depository Building

Though there is still a heated debate over just how many shots were fired in Dealey Plaza that day, most witnessed claimed to have heard three, with the first coming shortly after the motorcade turned onto Elm Street. It is believed that the first shot missed, as evidenced by a study of the Zapruder film that seems to indicate members of the motorcade reacting to the sound of a shot before the President suffered any injuries. Most witnesses also claimed the first shot occurred as the President was waving.

If so, the second shot fired hit the President in the upper back and penetrated his throat before exiting his body around the knot of his tie. According to the Warren Commission, this same bullet proceeded to strike Governor Conally in the armpit, crushing a rib and shattering his wrist upon exiting his body. Conspiracy theorists openly dismiss the notion that the same bullet wreaked such damage on both men and refer to it as the "Magic Bullet" theory, but a look at the Zapruder film shows Kennedy reacting to his injury and Connally reacting to his simultaneously.

At the time, Jackie initially thought there was a malfunction in the vehicle, not realizing what had happened until Governor Connally turned around and screamed. At that moment, Jackie created an indelible image by leaning in closer to her husband, whose hands had bunched up into fists as he was grasping at his neck. The concerned First Lady put her arm around the President, recognizing that he was wounded. At that moment, a second shot entered the rear of the President's head and shattered his skull, spraying blood, bone fragments and brain matter all over the vehicle's interior and on Mrs. Kennedy.

Jackie, in shock, then proceeded to start crawling along the back of the vehicle as Secret Service Agent Clint Hill, who had started running toward the limousine upon hearing shots fired, jumped onto the back and told her to get down in the seat. Hill later said he thought Mrs. Kennedy was reaching for a piece of the President's skull that had been blasted off in the attack. As the limousine quickly sped off underneath the underpass, Jackie reportedly told Mr. and Mrs. Connally, "They have killed my husband. I have his brains in my hand."

Over 100 witnesses in attendance that day would be interviewed, and though most believed that they heard the shots come from the vicinity of the School Book Depository Building, a strong percentage thought they heard shots fired from the grassy knoll that lined the Plaza. Some of the people were so sure that they scattered across the area in search of a sniper, though none was found. Others chose to lie down on the grass with their children as the shots were fired, afraid that more bullets were coming.

The grassy knoll

With two grievously wounded men in the limousine, the President's motorcade predictably sped toward the nearest hospital, the University of Texas Parkland Hospital. Kennedy immediately entered a Trauma Room, where doctors began operating, but the emergency room doctors had realized from the beginning that his condition was "moribund", another way of saying he was dead on arrival. Regardless, they performed a traecheotomy and CPR, but to no avail. Meanwhile, the First Lady demanded to be let into the operating room, wanting to be with her husband when he died. Though she was initially denied, doctors relented and allowed her in. A priest was also called in to administer last rites. At 1:00 p.m. Central Standard Time, the President was declared dead. With that, Mrs. Kennedy put her wedding ring on her husband's finger and he was loaded into a casket. Governor Connally, meanwhile, was undergoing surgery for his wounds, and was not able to hear of the official news that the President had died.

Aside from the spectators who turned out to greet Kennedy and his wife at Dealey Plaza, some of the first to hear the news were those listening to Dallas radio. At 12:39, people listening to *The Rex Jones Show* were among the first to hear about the shooting: "This KLIF Bulletin from Dallas: Three shots reportedly were fired at the motorcade of President Kennedy today near the downtown section. KLIF News is checking out the report, we will have further reports, stay tuned." Television viewers who were watching a show on the local ABC affiliate found out around 12:45, when a news director who had been in Dealey Plaza ran back to deliver an impromptu news bulletin: Good afternoon, ladies and gentlemen. You'll excuse the fact that I am out of breath, but about 10 or 15 minutes ago a tragic thing from all indications at this point has happened in the city of Dallas. "Let me quote to you this, and I'll... you'll excuse me if I am out of breath. A bulletin, this is from the United Press from Dallas: 'President Kennedy and Governor John Connally have been cut down by assassins' bullets in downtown Dallas.'"

Outside of Dallas, the first people to find out about the shooting were those watching the soap opera *As the World Turns* on CBS. In the middle of the show, just minutes after Kennedy had been shot, Walter Cronkite cut in with a CBS News Bulletin announcing that President Kennedy had been shot at and was severely wounded: "Here is a bulletin from CBS News. In Dallas, Texas, three shots were fired at President Kennedy's motorcade in downtown Dallas. The first reports say that President Kennedy has been seriously wounded by this shooting. More details just arrived. These details about the same as previously: President Kennedy shot today just as his motorcade left downtown Dallas. Mrs. Kennedy jumped up and grabbed Mr. Kennedy, she called 'Oh, no!' The motorcade sped on. United Press says that the wounds for President Kennedy perhaps could be fatal. Repeating, a bulletin from CBS News, President Kennedy has been shot by a would-be assassin in Dallas, Texas. Stay tuned to CBS News for further details."

The news began to spread across offices and schools across the country, with teary-eyed teachers having to inform their schoolchildren of the shooting in Dallas. Most Americans left school and work early and headed home to watch the news. Even the normally stoic Cronkite couldn't hide his emotions. Acting Press Secretary Malcolm Kilduff had the unfortunate job of officially announcing the President's death to the world, which he did that day at 1:33 p.m. A few minutes later, around 1:40 p.m. CST, misty eyed and with his voice choked up, Cronkite delivered the news that the president was dead.

About a half hour later, the President's body, along with Vice President Johnson and Mrs. Kennedy, boarded Air Force One to return to Washington. With the President dead, Johnson was sworn in aboard Air Force One at around 2:38 p.m. that afternoon, with the former First Lady at his side in a blood-stained dress. Jackie continued to wear her pink outfit as an intentional reminder of what had just happened, and both she and the outfit were still full of the President's blood. Though she had washed her face and hair (something she later claimed she regretted), parts of John's skull were still on her.

The swearing-in was a first in many respects: never before had a President been sworn in to office in Texas, or by a woman. Judge Sarah Hughes was the most accessible judge in the area ready and able to swear-in the President. In his first official statement as president, Johnson told the shocked nation, "This is a sad time for all people. We have suffered a loss that cannot be weighed. For me, it is a deep, personal tragedy. I know the world shares the sorrow that Mrs. Kennedy and her family bear. I will do my best; that is all I can do. I ask for your help and God's."

Chapter 4: Chaos in Dallas

According to official investigations, about 90 seconds after shots were fired a young man named Lee Harvey Oswald was spotted by a policeman in the School Book Depository Building, but he did not seem out of breath and the police noticed no rifle or anything that would have made him seem suspicious. They let him pass after he was identified as an employee, and he allegedly exited the building around 12:33 p.m.

Just minutes later, at 12:40, Oswald boarded a city bus but quickly disembarked due to heavy traffic and took a cab home instead. He arrived there almost at precisely 1:00 p.m., just as President Kennedy's death was being pronounced.

Minutes before Oswald got home, a description of the potential shooter back in Dealey Plaza had been given to Dallas police. Howard Brennan, who had been sitting across the street from the School Book Depository Building, had already told police that he heard a shot come from above as the motorcade passed him, and when he looked up he saw a man with a rifle taking a shot from the corner window on the sixth floor of the building. He also claimed to have seen the same man looking out the same window a few minutes earlier. Brennan gave the best description he could, and it was already being broadcast to Dallas police officers within 15 minutes of the shooting. Around the same time, an employee at the Depository Building notified police that one of the men he supervised at the Building, Lee Harvey Oswald, was missing. Police would quickly find a high-powered rifle belonging to Oswald near the corner window of the sixth floor, with boxes arranged to create a "sniper's nest".

Oswald's housekeeper reported that Oswald briskly left his home and began walking towards downtown. As he did so, a police officer named J.D. Tippitt pulled over to investigate Oswald around 1:15 p.m. Tippitt had been told by the owner of the Texas Book Depository that Oswald was the only man missing after the assassination. Tippitt, after pulling over, exited his car but was almost immediately shot and killed by Oswald.

Tippitt

A local shoe store owner saw the shooting and saw Oswald ducking in the alcove in his building. He later saw him enter a nearby theater without paying and notified the ticket booth at the theater, who notified police. Police arrived shortly after and confronted Oswald at 1:40 p.m. Oswald pulled a gun on the officer, but it misfired and he was arrested. As he was being taken away, he yelled loudly about police brutality.

Oswald being removed from the theater

As Oswald was brought into the police station for custody, reporters rattled him with questions. When asked if he killed the President, he said the question was the first time he'd heard of the President's death. He was also asked about his associations with the USSR. Investigations quickly unearthed the fact that Oswald had once been in the Marine Corps and was a proficient enough shooter that he was a sharpshooter during his time in the mid-'50s. He was also suspected of trying to assassinate retired U.S. Major General Edwin Walker presumably because of Walker's staunch anti-Communist views.

That day, stunned Americans wondered if the assassination was a Soviet conspiracy, a Cuban conspiracy, or the actions of a lone nut. Naturally, the interrogation of Oswald was dominated by those same concerns. Over the following days, police interrogated Oswald first about Tippitt's death and then the assassination of Kennedy. He could not keep his story straight when asked to account for himself at the time of President Kennedy's assassination. At one point, he said he was eating lunch, at another that he was working on the third floor. Amid conspiracies that Oswald was working for the Soviets, he was asked if he was a communist, to which he replied, "No, I am a Marxist." All throughout, Oswald insisted he was a "patsy", but investigators were certain he was lying. Oswald denied shooting Kennedy or Tippitt, even though his sniper rifle was found at the Depository and bullet casings at the scene of Tippitt's murder were traced back to the revolver found on Oswald when he was arrested in the theater. Oswald claimed two photographs of him holding both murder weapons were fakes, and he denied the statement by his co-worker that he had carried a long and heavy package to work on the morning of November

On Sunday, November 24th, Oswald was being led through the Dallas jail's basement to be transferred to the county jail nearby, but a Dallas nightclub owner named Jack Ruby shot Oswald in the abdomen as he was being transferred. Oswald was taken to the same hospital where Kennedy was pronounced dead, where he was declared dead at 1:07 p.m. on November 24th, almost exactly 48 hours after the President was declared dead. Jack Ruby was quickly arrested, and right away the media began speculating that he had killed Oswald as part of a broader conspiracy.

Ruby approaches Oswald

Chapter 5: A State Funeral

After being flown back to Washington, Kennedy's body underwent an autopsy at the Bethesda Medical Center. Meanwhile, the Commanding General of the Military District of Washington began planning the President's state funeral. At Bethesda, the President's body was also prepared for burial.

President Kennedy's body was brought back to the White House, where it rested in repose in the East Room for 24 hours, draped in an American flag. Up to that time, Jacquie Kennedy had been with the body during each step of the voyage, but she agreed to leave it in the East Room alone so long as a Catholic priest was by its side. Two Roman Catholic priests were called in from the nearby Catholic University of America and prayed at the side of the body, while military guards stood in formation around it. These hours in the East Room were for private viewings only.

The President's body in the East Room

The next day, the President's casket was taken in the same carriage that once carried Franklin Roosevelt's body to the Capitol. About 300,000 people came to Washington to watch the procession from the White House to the Capitol, which included a horse drawn carriage. There, he lay in state in the Capitol Rotunda, and over an 18-hour span, a public viewing flooded the

Capitol with grieving citizens.

The viewing ended on Monday, November 25, at 9:30 a.m., with the President's funeral beginning promptly at 10:30. Because no funeral plans were drawn up prior to Kennedy's death, the precedent set by Abraham Lincoln's assassination was used as a model. Dignitaries from around the world and within the U.S. attended Kennedy's funeral, including all surviving presidents except Herbert Hoover, who was too ill to attend (and died months later).

The President's body was brought from the Capitol to St. Matthew's Cathedral for a complete funeral. Throughout the funeral, brothers Ted and Bobby played important and visible roles in helping lead both the Kennedy family and the nation through the grieving process. They were with Jackie at all critical moments and helped organize and ensure that the state funeral went as smoothly as possible. The three of them had to visit the rotunda and escort the President's body out of the Capitol.

Mrs. Kennedy walked with both of her children as the procession moved to St. Matthew's. Famously, she instructed John Kennedy Jr. to salute his father's coffin as it passed. Sadly, his third birthday, November 25, 1963, coincided with the funeral. Deemed too young to attend the burial, the salute would be John Jr.'s final goodbye to his father.

After the funeral Mass, President Kennedy's body was taken to Arlington National Cemetery for burial. At the end of the burial service, approximately 3:34 p.m., Jackie lit the eternal flame that continues to burn above the President's grave to this day. That famous tribute to Kennedy's memory was his wife's idea.

The internment of Kennedy at Arlington

President Kennedy's burial was the end of an era. Mrs. Kennedy and her children remained in the White House until December 5th, when they departed for a final time.

Chapter 6: Initial Investigations

Both the local Dallas Police Department and the FBI conducted early investigations of the Kennedy Assassination in its immediate aftermath. The Dallas Police were joined by the FBI and members of the Secret Service during the only interrogations of accused assassin Lee Harvey Oswald, who spoke little and never admitted to killing the President. A test was conducted to detect the presence of gunpowder on Oswald and turned up positive for his hands.

J. Edgar Hoover, director of the FBI, also conducted an investigation of the assassination in the immediate aftermath. Their investigation ended less than a month after the assassination and concluded that three bullets were fired: the first hit the President's shoulder, the second hit Governor Connally, and the third struck the President in the head, fatally wounding him. This would be contradicted in critical detail by the findings of the Warren Commission, and in 1979 the House Select Committee on Assassinations would declare in its findings that the FBI failed to adequately investigate whether Oswald's participation was part of a broader conspiracy.

In the days after the President's assassination, Americans across the country were on edge. Was this part of a broader conspiracy to sabotage the government? Were the Soviets involved and would this be a tactic they could employ repeatedly in the future? Lee Harvey Oswald's death only added a stronger shroud of uncertainty over the incident. He had, after all, claimed to be a Marxist before his own murder. Having died, however, the world would never know the truth of Lee Harvey Oswald, or if he was even the lone murderer.

Threats from within the country also surfaced as a topic of conversation. The rapid rise in power of both the CIA and the FBI in recent decades made many Americans suspicious of their role. Reportedly, two CIA agents were in Dallas at the time of the shooting. Why were they there? Were they involved or somehow complicit in the assassination of the President? Was American democracy unravelling at the seams?

While many of these questions were thrown off as outlandish and unsubstantiated, the conversation continued to broil, perturbing the American public. The death of John F. Kennedy was the first assassination in the modern era, with television and radio to announce it to the world in real time. Americans were rightly shocked.

Shortly after becoming President, Johnson hoped to end the conspiracies swirling around the Kennedy assassination by appointing the Warren Commission, a committee of prominent individuals charged with investigating the death of the President. Supreme Court Chief Justice Earl Warren was its chairman, thus the name "Warren Commission." Moreover, in the immediate aftermath of the assassination Johnson feared for his own life, believing the death could be part of a Soviet plot. He wanted concrete answers quickly.

The most famous and scrutinized investigation of the assassination started within a week, with the Warren Commission being established on November 29th, 1963. Along with Warren, the Commission consisted of seven very notable members of the American political community: Senator Richard Russell, a Georgia Democrat for whom a Senate Office Building is today named; Senator John Sherman Cooper, a Kentucky Republican; Representative Hale Boggs, the House Majority Leader; Representative Gerald Ford, the House Minority Leader and future U.S. President; CIA Director Allen Welsh Dulles; and John J. McCloy, former President of the World Bank. The group was diverse, wide-ranging and powerful.

The Warren Commission presenting its findings to President Johnson

The Commission spent an entire year trying to sort out the facts of the Kennedy assassination, and much of the investigation was conducted privately. As such, despite the fact its findings would be made public, there is little knowledge of the conversations that went on behind closed doors. A total of 94 testimonies took place with Dallas residents and others who were present on the day of the assassination, and perhaps the most critical piece of evidence unearthed from the Warren Commission was the famous Zapruder Film. The film was shot near the grassy knoll in Dealey Plaza by a private citizen, Abraham Zapruder, and it caught the assassination on video, allowing the world to rewatch and investigate. Since he filmed from an elevated position, it has become the most memorable visual evidence, and it captured the fatal shot in excruciatingly grisly detail.

In the end, after a year of testimony, the Warren Commission issued its report to the President as the Warren Report on September 24, 1964. In it, the Warren Report contradicted some of the Dallas Police Department's earlier claims about the events of November 22, 1963. Warren agreed that three shots were fired, but they disagreed that all three hit either President Kennedy or Governor Connally. Instead, the Warren Report insisted that the second bullet hit Kennedy in the back, going through his throat to then strike Connally, and the third hit Kennedy in the head. The Warren Commission concluded the first bullet missed, contrary to the Dallas Police Report's investigation.

On other points, the Commission agreed with Dallas police and the FBI. For example, both thought there was only one gunman - likely Lee Harvey Oswald - and that he fired from the Texas Book Depository.

When the Warren Commission first commenced, many thought it might do more harm than good. While speculation about the Kennedy assassination was swirling, commentators thought a formal commission might be a lightning bolt for criticism, allowing for conspiracy theories to spread more widely. As it was, some of the findings were doubted by President Johnson, Bobby Kennedy, and even some of the Commission's members, all of whom expressed skepticism about certain points off the record.

As a result, a series of other lesser known investigations were conducted to try to discern the facts about the Kennedy assassination. The first of these came out of the White House and was known colloquially as the Rockefeller Commission. In 1975, President Gerald Ford had Vice President Nelson Rockefeller lead a commission called the United States President's Commission on CIA Activities within the United States. The purpose, as the name describes, was not entirely and exclusively to investigate Kennedy; instead, the Commission was charged with unraveling the full role of CIA operations within American borders.

With speculation about the role of the CIA in Kennedy's death swirling, however, the Commission could not avoid the topic. Specifically, the group looked at whether or not CIA operatives (and later Nixon henchman) E. Howard Hunt and Frank Sturgis were in Dallas on the day of the assassination and if they were involved. Some suggested that these men assassinated Kennedy and used Oswald as a cover up. Others thought Oswald was the assassin, but conspired with the CIA. The President's Commission, however, concluded that there was no substance to either of these claims and dismissed them.

The next committee to investigate the incident came out of the U.S. Senate. The Church Committee, known more formally as the United States Senate Select Committee to Study Governmental Operations with Respect to Intelligence Activities, was chaired by Senator Frank Church in 1975. Its express purpose was also not to investigate Kennedy but to survey the CIA and FBI in the wake of Watergate. The Commission hoped to better understand the role of the organizations in American life.

Unfortunately, the Church Committee came to a whole new conclusion: the FBI and CIA investigations of the Kennedy Assassination had been deficient and both organizations withheld valuable information from the Warren Commission. Gerald Ford, who was part of the Warren Commission, noted the CIA had kept certain evidence away from the Warren Commission because the Commission's investigation put "certain classified and potentially damaging operations in danger of being exposed." But naturally, conspiracy theorists, now completely unsure who to believe, began to think up more fanciful conspiracies than ever before.

Due to a whole new round of assassinations in the late 1960s, particularly the murders of Bobby Kennedy and Martin Luther King Jr., the House of Representatives decided to investigate assassinations for itself with yet another Committee. This time, the committee's purpose was explicit: assassinations. The United States House Select Committee on Assassinations took all that had been done and re-investigated it, opening new wounds again in 1976. Rather than putting conspiracy theories to rest, this new committee only lit the flames of existing theorists.

The Committee agreed with some findings of the Warren Commission but added others that were vague and left the doors open to wild ideas. First, the Committee agreed that Lee Harvey Oswald fired the fatal shot at the President and that he fired three times, hitting the President twice. However, their second conclusion was the one that proved most contested: the Commission agreed that it could not rule out the possibility of a second gunman on the grassy knoll. The House Committee believed that a Dictabelt audio recording of radio transmissions made by the Dallas Police Department Acoustic suggested that 4 shots were fired, not 3. Thus, the acoustic evidence left a "high probability" that a second gunman was present at the time of the shooting. The committee, however, was unable to identify a possible identity for the second gunman. Moreover, in subsequent years other scientists have refuted the acoustic evidence the House Committee relied on, claiming the Dictabelt recording of radio transmissions made by the Dallas Police Department did not dispositively indicate bullets were fired from elsewhere.

Among all its findings, one of the conclusions offered up by the House offered more fuel for the fire. It stated that the President's death was likely the result of a conspiracy, though it ruled out the participation of the Soviet Union, Cuba, or members of a government agency. The report went on to suggest that, while as a whole groups like organized crime and anti-Castro groups were not involved in Kennedy's death, individual members of these groups may have acted on their own.

Despite their controversial findings, the Commission apparently still sought to undermine conspiracy theories by stressing that the investigation it conducted took place over a decade after the shooting and was thus not able to access the best evidence possible.

Documentation of the Warren Commission and the various other commissions were highly valued in light of the conflicting reports of the assassination, but the processes and events surrounding the evidence of assassination only further inflamed conspiracy theorists. The original Warren Commission submitted its report to the National Archives in 1964, and general National Archives policy at the time stipulated that the documents be sealed for 75 years, which would have kept them under wraps until 2039.

Such lack of transparency, however, outraged Americans who wanted to know more about the assassination of their President. The Freedom of Information Act of 1966 changed the policy in an effort to offer more transparency of government operations to citizens. Unfortunately, not all documents relating to the Kennedy Assassination were immediately released at this time.

To get the documents fully released to the public, yet another commission was needed. This time, the Assassination Records Review Board was created out of the the President John F. Kennedy Assassination Records Collection Act of 1992. The Act sought to release all documents relating to Kennedy's death amid controversy and conspiracy theory. A recently-released movie, titled simply *JFK*, was part of the controversy then swirling around the assassination.

Still not all documents were released, though about 98% were made public over the next few years. The remaining documents, with very few exceptions, are to go public by 2017.

Chapter 7: Conspiracies

John F. Kennedy was assassinated nearly 5 decades ago, but today an overwhelming number of Americans do not believe the information conveyed by the Warren Commission. What they *do* believe is less certain, but the vast majority of Americans do not believe that Lee Harvey Oswald acted alone in the assassination of John F. Kennedy. Undoubtedly, the conflicting information given by the various government commissions played a role in this public perception.

Researchers sifted through the evidence and investigations used by the various commissions, and found significant holes. This added fodder to the fire of conspiracy theorists. The first obvious disturbing problem with the Kennedy investigation involved the death of numerous critical witnesses. This included, of course, Lee Harvey Oswald himself, the accused assassin, who was murdered by Ruby before a trial. While many Americans could accept that Oswald was the lone shooter, they are more apt not to believe that Oswald was a lone nut who was then shot 48 hours later seemingly at random by another lone nut. Ruby's murder of Oswald seemed too unbelievable to not be tied to a larger conspiracy.

Other prominent deaths included a woman named Dorothy Kilgallen, a prominent American journalist who studied politics and organized crime. Reportedly, she had interviewed Jack Ruby, Lee Harvey Oswald's assassin, when he was on trial for killing Oswald. While this information might have been incredibly useful in uncovering the relationships between the various characters surrounding the assassination, Dorothy Kilgallen died mysteriously on November 8th, 1965, from an overdose of alcohol and barbiturates. Unfortunately, medical examiners were unable to determine whether her death was simply an accidental overdose or a suicide. This other mysterious element – why she died so suddenly just hours after appearing on television – added another layer of mystery to the Kennedy death. Was she killed as part of a cover up?

Even Jack Ruby's death came relatively early, of lung cancer in 1967. Considering his death came shortly after the President's, many suspected that he knew of his lung cancer in 1963, and that it motivated him to become involved in a cover up, knowing he would die before information could be divulged.

Other deaths in the Kennedy conspiracy included numerous Mafia members before 1970. This included as many as 10 people. Additionally, more people related to Jack Ruby died, incuding four of the showgirls who worked at his club. All of these deaths coming in a relatively short time span, related to organized crime or the figures known to be involved with the assassination, only hardened the views of conspiracy theorists.

The final major committee investigating Kennedy's death in the House opened a huge door for conspiracy theories by legitimizing the idea of multiple gunmen. To be an authentic "conspiracy," more than one person needed to be involved, so conspiracy theorists jumped on this evidence.

The Warren Commission concluded that the three shots fired at the President's motorcade took place within a 4.8 to 7 second timeframe, and most witnesses agreed that the shots were not evenly spaced out, with a noticeable delay between the first and second shots and a much smaller amount of time between the second and third shots. Given that Oswald was a former Marine with plenty of experience firing his own gun, people can accept that he could fire three shots in such a tight time frame, but if the acoustic evidence correctly suggested 4 shots were fired, it would have been impossible for the sniper in the School Book Depository Building to fire them all in 7 seconds. Furthermore, it's unclear why Oswald, who knew what he was doing with a high-powered rifle, would space out his shots unevenly. On top of that, Governor Connally himself suggested to the Warren Commission that, as the motorcade was being fired at, he thought more than one gunmen was firing. He reportedly told his wife "they're going to kill all of us!" as bullets were flying.

Of course, there were also plenty of witnesses on the ground – spectators eager to see the

President – had a different view of the assassination than the Warren Commission. Many in attendance at the time of the assassination thought the shots were fired from the famous grassy knoll along the President's route. The Warren Commission, on the other hand, discounted this theory, believing the bullets all came from the Texas Book Depository. Others believed that at least one shot came from the Dal-Tex Building, which was immediately across from the Texas Book Depository. Employees in that building reported that the shots they heard were loud enough to have been from their building.

Other evidence overlooked by the Warren Commission corresponds with a theory of multiple gunmen. The only spectator injured in the assassination, James Tague, was injured on his right cheek when a bullet ricocheted towards him. According to researchers, however, the trajectory of the bullet that struck Tague was not consistent with one fired from the Texas Book Depository.

All of these conflicted reports, when taken together, lead conspiracy theorists to believe that more than one gunman fired the shots that killed President Kennedy. How else could so many different people believe fundamentally different things about the events of November 22, 1963?

Aside from the belief that Oswald wasn't the only shooter, conspiracy theories have focused on several suspects. One major conspiracy theory suspect was a straightforward one: Lyndon Johnson, who notoriously did not get on well with Bobby Kennedy and felt isolated and powerless as John's Vice President. The theory is that he wanted the President dead so that he could occupy the White House.

The first time this idea gained major traction came in 1968 with a book titled *The Dark Side of Lyndon Baines Johnson*. The book posited that Lyndon Johnson led a ring of Dallas-area FBI members, CIA agents and police officials who conspired to assassinate the President. Johnson was from Texas, the site of Kennedy's death, so the book thought the site was fitting for the Johnson-motivated assassination.

In 2003, the Johnson debate reignited with a book titled *Blood, Money and Power*. This book gave a more elaborate explanation of Johnson's involvement. According to the book, he conspired with a Dallas-area lawyer friend and that the two worked out the placement of an associate on the 6th floor of the Texas Book Depository who later shot the President. Oil magnates paid the assassin, and they were rewarded with oil-positive legislation during Johnson's term.

Madeline Brown, who claimed to be Johnson's mistress, later said that she had firsthand knowledge of Johnson's involvement in Kennedy's assassination. Other figures also intervened to add fodder to the Johnson Conspiracy. Lee Harvey Oswald's surgeon at the Parkland Hospital reportedly spoke to Johnson on the phone as Oswald was entering the hospital. According to him, Johnson demanded a death-bed confession from Oswald, stating he killed the President. This, conspiracy theorists believe, indicated that Johnson wanted someone to cover up the assassination and silence any speculation about Johnson.

Most credible historians refute the Johnson conspiracy. On the contrary, many professional historians note Johnson had his own conspiracy theory; he thought the murder was the fault of Castro's Cuba. Despite these private beliefs, however, he tried to keep his beliefs quiet out of fear that making them public might ignite a Soviet-American nuclear war over the fate of Cuba.

The CIA and the FBI are together taken as the most suspicious government entities potentially involved with the Kennedy Assassination. Conspiracy theorists point to numerous pieces of evidence to implicate them.

The first major piece surrounds Lee Harvey Oswald's relationship to government agency. In the past, he had received suspicious preferential treatment that suggests something questionable. Oswald, an avowed communist, had previously moved to the Soviet Union but was allowed to repatriate to the United States after speaking with officials from the State Department. Such a move to the USSR and back to the U.S. was rare; at the time, Americans leaving for the USSR were viewed with extreme suspicion and were rarely allowed to return. Oswald, on the other hand, was allowed to return with an almost $500 repatriation loan to boot.

Other pieces of evidence allegedly chronicle a deep Oswald-CIA relationship. Just a week before the assassination, Oswald reportedly showed up at the Dallas FBI office and asked to speak with agent James Hosty. The Warren Commission knew of this relationship, but when it asked for letters of correspondence between Hosty and Oswald, Hosty had all of them destroyed by orders from his superiors. For this, Hosty was reprimanded and transferred to an office in Kansas City. Those who dismiss these conspiracy theories suggest that Oswald actually left a letter threatening to attack or bomb the FBI office.

Oswald had other relationships with the CIA and FBI. After being arrested in New Orleans in August of 1963, he asked to speak with an FBI agent and did so, which conspiracy theorists allege is highly unusual for someone arrested on a charge of disturbing the peace. He spoke for over an hour to Agent John Quigley.

Many who knew Oswald or were involved with the CIA thought Lee Harvey Oswald was an employee for the Agency. Members of the Tokyo CIA Office leaked to the press that Oswald had been sent to Russia as a spy in the 1950's. Even Oswald's mother stated that Oswald was sent to Russia "by the government" in 1959.

With this evidence, conspiracies diverge. Some suspect Oswald was hired by the CIA to kill the President. Others thought Oswald was not the assassin, but that the CIA used him as a scapegoat after he began to dissent from CIA activities.

Perhaps the most widely believed conspiracy theory, and certainly the least radical, is that President Kennedy was assassinated as part of a mob conspiracy. Those who believe this theory point to the fact that Attorney General Bobby Kennedy had been a thorn in the side of organized crime for over a decade, including during his brother's administration. It's also widely assumed that Jack Ruby, as a notorious Dallas nightclub owner, was in a line of business that would have possibly connected him to the criminal underworld. To conspiracy theorists, mob ties explain Ruby's actions better than the notion that he simply snapped and decided to try to kill Oswald in revenge for his assassination of the President.

Chapter 8: Legacy

Lincoln and Kennedy

As Americans tried to make sense of Kennedy's life and death, the mythology enveloping his presidency popped up quickly. Aside from the label of his presidency as Camelot, people looked to the links between Kennedy and another beloved assassinated President: Abraham Lincoln. One of the first major fascinations surrounding Kennedy's assassination focused on the seeming coincidences between the assassinations of John F. Kennedy and Abraham Lincoln. These have since become well known among Americans, even if they are full of exaggerations and easy to explain coincidences.

The first similarity between the two involved their political history. Lincoln was elected to Congress in 1846, Kennedy in 1946. Both men were runners-up for their party's Vice Presidential nomination in 1856 and 1956 respectively. Lincoln was elected President in 1860, Kennedy in 1960. As President, both had Vice Presidents with the last name Johnson: Lincoln had Andrew Johnson, Kennedy has Lyndon Johnson.

Other minor things surround the two men. Lincoln's Vice President was born in 1808, Kennedy's in 1908. Both suffered the death of a child in the White House, a rare occurrence in American history. Some people even point to the most basic coincidence, like the fact both Presidents also had seven letters in their last names.

Regarding their assassinations, the similarities are also noteworthy. Both Presidents were assassinated by men whose full names consisted of 15 letters and who are known by their full names (although this is not unique among assassins, as in the case of John Lennon's killer, Mark David Chapman): John Wilkes Booth and Lee Harvey Oswald. Both Presidents were assassinated on a Friday by being shot in the back of the head in the presence of their wives.

Lincoln was shot in Ford's Theater, while Kennedy was shot in a Lincoln vehicle made by Ford Auto, and both assassins were killed before they could be tried. Worse, both men sympathized with an organization or body that was an enemy of the United States: in Booth's case, it was the Confederate States of America, in Oswald's, the Soviet Union.

And of course, Kennedy's coffin rested on the Lincoln Catafalque, which was originally used for Lincoln's coffin in 1865 and is still used for state funerals.

Lincoln Catafalque

These mysterious coincidences began appearing in the mainstream public as early as 1964. The American people, already unsure what to make of the Kennedy assassination, had found yet another aspect of Kennedy's life and death to envelop in mystery, intrigue, and mythology.

Remembering November 22, 1963

November 22nd, 1963, much like September 11th, 2001, and December 7th, 1941, is a date that any American old enough to have lived through it remembers vividly. Just about anyone above the age of 5 can remember where they were and what they were doing when they learned of the first assassination of a President in the modern era. Unlike previous assassinations – the most recent being William McKinley's in 1901 – Kennedy's was broadcast live over radio and television. Television reporters teared up as they delivered the news. And unlike other Presidents, whose faces were pasted in newspapers with no voice or sound, Kennedy was a well-known celebrity. His presidency was the first to be dominated by multiple forms of real-time media, making his death feel that much more intimate and tragic to Americans.

Furthermore, the fact that Kennedy's assassination practically played out in real time, with only minutes separating the assassination and news reports about it, has likely contributed to the conspiracy theories surrounding his death. Unlike other assassinations, Americans were able to study and reflect on the events for themselves rather than read a predetermined story in their local newspaper. By delivering the assassination via radio and television in real time, reporters did not have all the facts, giving the American people the impression that much was unknown and that a conspiracy or cover-up was possible.

Other social factors contribute to the mystery of John F. Kennedy's assassination. In an era when the American government was becoming more powerful and invasive than ever before, Americans were increasingly skeptical of entities like the CIA and FBI. They became good scapegoats for the greatest American tragedy since World War II.

In the end, Americans are left to decide for themselves who killed John F. Kennedy. With many of the prominent players now gone and the evidence slim, perhaps the country will never know how exactly its President died. Either way, the event served as a significant moment in the history of the United States, and it has come to symbolize the turbulent transition from the tranquil '50s to the troublesome '60s.

Made in the USA
Las Vegas, NV
14 May 2023

72059044R00046